Basic Information

Application

Technology

Introduction

Type is alive – across generations even, with every era celebrating its own technical accomplishments. Innovations were created and developed further, the true and tested was refined. Font styles appeared and disappeared.

Type has become replaceable, yet every era remains reflected in the typefaces that were developed and used in it. With the globalization of our world cultural exchange in every sector started to take place across national borders and continents. The advent of computers revolutionized the entire written communication process to its core. In conjunction with this, a second medium has developed for conveying text – the monitor with all its drawbacks and advantages. Today, we all consume, whether intentional or not, electronic texts, i.e. fonts. Whether at the cash register of the supermarket, when using various types of tellers and vending machines, on mobile and smartphones, on the tablet, or on computers and laptops.

Since the triumphant success of the Internet it seems as if the tradition of constantly evolving fonts has come to a standstill for the first time. This is not because no new typefaces are being created – rather to the contrary. It is easier than ever to create a typeface of your own. The technical possibilities for this seem unlimited. Anyone who wants to generate a typeface today, requires only a font editor and access to the Internet, in contrast to earlier times when special skills were required for drawing the letters by hand, cutting the punches, and then casting the letters. When it comes to distribution and sales there are also entirely new options. Nevertheless, the impression remains that the development of fonts for the

Web is stagnant. Actually, this is not the case as it was the technology lagged behind for a long time. Even though until 2009, the same ten so-called core fonts were mainly used for web pages, this was only because they were the only fonts that displayed well on monitors given the technical possibilities of the time. For a long time, the major problem was the fact that fonts could only be embedded on the Web and rendered on the browser if they were actually loaded on the computers of the website operator and the user. This is why only those ten core fonts were available online, which Apple and Windows agreed to provide with all their operating systems.

Today, luckily, this has changed due to new technologies and developments. After years of fidgeting and fussing, designers have finally reached a point at which they are able to use a great variety of fonts with improved technology. The universe of web fonts and typefaces available on the Web is literally exploding. Finally, thanks to web services such as Typekit, FontShop, Webtype and many others it is becoming increasingly easy to use fonts on the Web. We are no longer reliant on the font existing on the computers of users. Instead, we can access extensive font databases. What is more, the many partnerships among providers and font foundries allow the great variety of options available today. Nevertheless, experienced print designers in particular have many questions when deal-

niggli

Overlap
Web & Typography

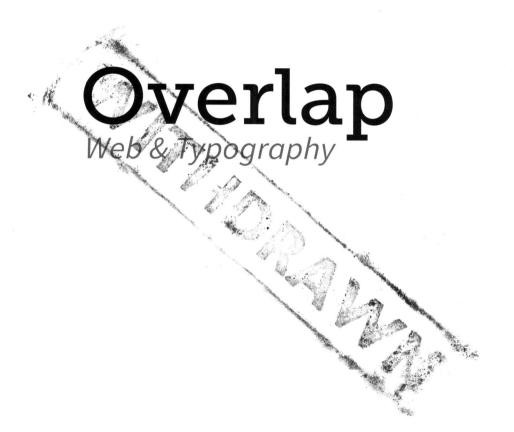

Jana Kemmer
Tabea Hartwich

Imprint/Contents

The Deutsche Nationalbibliothek lists this publication in the Deutsche Nationalbibliografie; detailed bibliographic data are available on the Internet at http://dnb.dnb.de

ISBN 978-3-7212-0946-4
© 2016 Niggli, imprint of bnb media gmbh, Zurich
1. Auflage 2016

Editing: **Sophie Steybe**
Text & layout: **Jana Kemmer & Tabea Hartwich**
Translation: **Cosima Talhouni**

www.niggli.ch

Acknowledgements

Jana and **Tabea** would like to thank Professor Andreas Teufel and Professor Daniel Utz for their support of the Bachelor's thesis, which was the trigger for this book. They would also like to thank Adi and Erika for their constant proofreading, Julius, whose HTML introduction many years ago allowed them to eventually write this book, and Niggli Publishing for the opportunity of implementing this book.

ing with web typography for the first time. To prevent them from resorting to the old habits and using only the core fonts, but instead dealing with the available variety and realizing what they should look out for, this book offers a comprehensive overview of everything that is required for handling typography on the Web.

Starting with the history of on-screen fonts, via the most popular contemporary font formats and their differences as well as the problems caused by different rasterizer systems, the chapter "Basic Information" presents the most important background information.

The chapter "Application" then delves into details. It explains the criteria that give fonts a readability advantage on the Web as well as what adjustments should be made and observed in a text in addition to the font selection to guarantee its optimal use. An overview of the different types of text on the Web helps gain a better impression of how different texts are read on screen media. The presentation of a selection of fonts that were analyzed based on different criteria shows how a simple systematic approach can be used to quickly test a font for its usability on the Web.

The final chapter deals with the basic embedding of fonts as well as some more detailed characteristics of microtypography on the Web and the use of fonts in the responsive sector. It also introduces tools that may come in handy for quick testing during the selection of a font.

Yet there remain areas in which important improvements need to be made and the technology will probably also continue to evolve. It is therefore important to rethink the rules set up in this book and to constantly deal with the topic of typography on the Web. A great number of blogs and Internet sites such as Smashing magazine or thenextweb (TNW) are valuable sources for keeping up to date. The sweeping approach of this book in presenting the most important basic information for the wide field of web typography should not be treated as a rigid set of rules and regulations, but is intended to offer an introduction to the subject and lay a foundation for better and more deliberate handling of fonts on screens – for a more diverse World Wide Web for all.

History

To get a better understanding of the development of web fonts within the past few years, it is a good idea to have a look at the history and early days of digital fonts. This provides an insight into the innovations and milestones that shaped the fonts found on the Web today.

In the 1960s, research institutions began to attempt to digitally recreate character shapes, or glyphs. The characters consisted of mathematically described curves. These could already be used on computers and even printed out. However, the memory capacities required for the bits[1] that were needed for the encoding were so large that the use of these bitmap fonts only became practical in the 1970s. At this time the introduction of semiconductor memory reduced the price of memory space.

In 1968, OCR-A was developed, the first font visually recognized by computers that met the criteria set by the U.S. Bureau of Standards, where OCR stands for Optical Character Recognition. In 1973, Adrian Frutiger developed OCR-B, which was declared a global standard at the time. It was primarily used for official forms and the recognition of expiry dates, for example in the pharmaceutical sector.

Between 1970 and 1975, the first "microcomputer," the "Altair 8800" by Edvard Roberts, conquered the US market. The first build-it-yourself computer kit that was affordable for household use, it caused a computer euphoria that began primarily in California. Subsequently in May 1979, seven American universities in cooperation with the NSF (National Science Foundation) introduced their own civil data network "CSNet"[2] for the exchange of text data, based on an already existing military network. Within a single decade, by the late 1970s, typesetting systems based on microcomputers (phototypesetting), which were initially optical, then photomechanical[3], replaced the 500-year-old metal typography. The systems were also known as "cold" printing systems as they no longer consisted of physically composed lines of metal type that were statically arranged as in the Linotype machine, from which the company that invented it later derived its name. In phototypesetting there were less mechanical limitations. It was now possible to combine characters or even distort fonts. Phototypesetting was an important factor in the development of digitized fonts by allowing, among other functions, the adjustment of space within character, which is known as kerning today. At the same time, this technology also had a few disadvantages. For example, in general, composition edges could not be influenced, while manual spacing or character pair kerning were not possible. These problems are still found in web typesetting today. The template exposure was photomechanical, which is why the method was called "phototypesetting".

Phototypesetting was primarily used to create templates that were then reproduced in offset printing or rotogravure printing. Toward the end of the phototypesetting era in the late 1980s, phototypesetting systems ran on SUN workstations, which allowed a type of postscript output. At the time, SUN (Stanford University Network) was a project for the networking of the library computers of Stan-

Monotype OCR-A Extended

Altair 8800 computer

ford University. This phototypesetting development already contained basic computer graphics and Electronic Page Setting (CEPS). It paved the way for the subsequent desktop publishing (DTP). It is interesting to note that at the time of phototypesetting it was already possible to digitize fonts by breaking individual letters down into individual controllable pixels. In the photo-electric variation of phototypesetting this was implemented via light or laser composition in which the character was not created by a template but rather by a cathode ray tube or laser beam.

Commodore VIC-20

The fonts of the first computers that were available for home use, such as the Commodore VIC-20, were known as bitmap fonts or pixel fonts. The graphic block look of each glyph, for which only 8x8 pixels were available, is due to the limited processing power available in the 1970s and 1980s. Basically, the characters consisted of collections of raster images that had to be created separately for every glyph of every font in each size. In theory, the number of possible font sizes was unlimited, however, as the memory of PCs at the time was not enough, most bitmap fonts were only available in frequently used sizes. Some applications still use these fonts to this day. For example, teletext on televisions as you can recognize.

As the manufacturers and the industry were well aware of the limitations of pixel fonts they aimed to find ways to overcome them. The milestone development in this regard was vector fonts, or outline fonts. Between 1980 and 1982, John Warnock founded "Adobe Systems", a software company which developed in the mid-1980s in cooperation with Apple, Aldus and Linotype modern desktop publishing (DTP). While Apple introduced the first fully graphic-based computer (Macintosh), Adobe contributed the page description language PostScript, which could create and read fonts in vectors. Aldus contributed the layout-compatible program PageMaker, and Linotype provided the first PostScript fonts.

Pixelfont/bitmap font on an Apple II computer

The printed materials created with this process were initially often belittled as they were inferior to the ones created with the standard printing methods, which was primarily due to the low printer resolution of the time.

Nevertheless, the new method constituted a milestone as the combination of Apple's laser writer printers with the PostScript fonts of Adobe allowed Adobe to establish its PostScript format as a standard in the printing sector and later to use the first vector-based fonts, the so-called Type 1 fonts, to create an industrial standard for the vector-based description of fonts.

In 1984 CSNet was converted in the USA to the TCP/IP-based "NSFNet". This change gave all US universities access to the "net". From the mid-1980s to the mid-1990s, many mostly geo-local networks were integrated around the world. In Germany, this took place in 1989. In the early 1990s, the "World Wide Web", which was developed by British scientist Tim Berners Lee in Bern, Switzerland was established. Its initial aim was to facilitate the exchange of research findings. Lee may have been already aware at the time that the collection of data available to the general public, which he was hoping to establish, would develop in such a rapid way.

In the mid-1990s, the World Wide Web began to be used for marketing purposes when Amazon and eBay went online. The use of the Web for marketing purposes led to a demand for a more attractive look. First browser versions could now recreate tables while Adobe continued to further develop the Post-Script font format. Simultaneously, Microsoft and Apple developed another font format called "TrueType". Based on this format, Microsoft commissioned a number of web-suitable fonts in which the focus was on optimal screen presentation. From 1996, Microsoft tried to establish the "core fonts for the web" as the standard for use on the Internet, but abandoned the project in 2002 and later the fonts were made available for free of charge download for Windows and Mac operating systems. Abandonment of the project and thus the free availability of the fonts led to their global distribution at the time. Some of these core fonts, which are also known as web safe fonts, are still used today. Most prominently Arial and Verdana are well known and widely used on the Web today, even among computer users who have nothing to do with professional DTP. In contrast, for example, Impact is rarely found on the Web today, for valid reasons to be quite honest, and, following an initial hype in the 1990s, ComicSans is luckily found less and less on the Web (and in print).

The historical logo of the World Wide Web, created by Robert Cailliau

"The World Wide Web is a large-scale hyper-media initiative for information sharing with the aim of providing general access to a large collection of documents."

Tim Berners-Lee

*Diatype machine of
Berthold AG*

From the mid-1980s to the mid-1990s the computer font formats PostScript and TrueType significantly altered the world of fonts. They rang in the start of the digitization of practically all fonts that were ever designed. Companies like Adobe began to rapidly expand their font libraries and new companies such as Bitstream[6] or FontShop AG[7] (cofounded by Erik Spiekermann) were established. Traditional internationally operating companies such as Linotype, who contributed significantly to the development of DTP, along with the Monotype Imaging Inc. foundries were among the few leading foundries and phototypesetting providers to hold their ground in the era of DTP. Others, such as the Berthold AG[10], which had created classic fonts including Akzidenz-Grotesk, Baskerville and Bodoni were not able to do so. The foundry closed its offices in Berlin in 1993 after declaring bankruptcy even though in 1960 it had developed the "Diatype", one of the first successful phototypesetting machines. They did not participate in the DTP era.

In the following years, new types of foundries emerged. These included Emigre[11], Font Bureau[12], Typekit[13], Fontdeck[14], to name just a few. *(for more information see the chapter Providers and Licenses, p. 30)*

 In December 1996 the first Cascading Style Sheet (CSS1) was introduced, with which contents could be structurally divided and design templates created. A little time later, in summer 1998, the follow-up version CSS2 was published. However, since both versions were not mature enough to allow independent designs, some users resorted to imbedding GIF graphics to create a typography that was in sync with the design.

From 1998 to 2005, the new "Flash" technology seemed to be a viable option as it allowed complete page layouts, design freedom, the free use of any type of fonts and the embedding of 'stylish' animations. However, it lost in popularity with the emergence of increasingly dynamic portals and User Generated Content[15]. Flash became obsolete no later than 2003 when another updated version CSS2.1 was published, which allowed storage of contents and presentation of information in separate files, which was a quantum leap for the complex layout design that we consider standard today. While Flash remains in use today, the first leading websites quickly switched to CSS layouts and the rest soon followed.

Web 2.0 design

From 2005, the standard became "Web 2.0-Design". JavaScript returned and opened a whole new range of possibilities together with CSS3 and HTML. The new focus was on large-scale minimalist shapes and the postcard format was discarded. Large headlines, increased use of color and gradients, as well as the utilization of the entire viewport[16] created a new style of web design.

In 2008 there was a turn-around for the use of web fonts initiated by the publication of Safari 3.1. Apple reintroduced the old @font-face rule. This rule had failed ten years earlier but could now be successfully implemented with the improved screen display technology. This rule provided the option of adding fonts to the font database that varies on every operating system. Since that time, the Post-Script technology has been included as standard the in Mac OS X. In Windows it is called ClearType and has been activated from Windows Vista.

Between 2008 and 2012 there were a number of milestones that can now be considered basic. The new font format WOFF (Web Open Font Format, published in 2009) gives web fonts a technically functional and license-free future. All current browsers, except for the pre-installed Android browser, support the WOFF format. In addition, all current browsers, except for InternetExplorer also support the presentation of TrueType fonts and True-Type-based OpenType fonts.

(for more information see the chapter Font Formats, p. 14)

Screenshot font embedding via @fontface

The emergence of the numerous web font embedding options and the optimization of fonts for presentation on screen allow designers today to once gain resort to traditional typographic rules from the print sector when handling fonts. At the same time, the various licensing models and the development of fonts that were specifically created for on-screen use offers new solutions and style options for using fonts in design processes on digital output media. Google's free font portal Webfonts significantly contributed to this development as it has made web fonts generally accessible.

Facilitated online purchasing and selling through downloads and web hosting[17] of web fonts today allows even small labels to offer licenses of their fonts. A veritable flood of fonts offers more choices today than ever before. Large and small font foundries are currently working on optimizing and licensing the major part of their font catalogs for use on the Web, as well as establishing interesting new fonts that are developed specifically for on-screen use. However, it continues to be essential to carefully select fonts as not all fonts that are available and can be embedded on the Web are actually suitable for each individual application. Currently a variety of licensing models are undergoing a test phase among customers and providers themselves.

Time-based licensing models, the purchase of entire typefaces or individual fonts, coupled with web hosting solutions and the offer of free fonts today offer a large selection of very varied licensing concepts and services. Providers such as "Fontslice" and "SkyFonts™" occasionally test completely new models in

Today's selection of fonts

which the users purchase font licenses for a specific period of time (web-click) or purchase only parts of a font (Fontslice). Apparently Fontslice was not successful and has already discontinued its service, which was only available as a beta version.

In the meantime, SkyFonts™ was purchased by Monotype and has been integrated into the font libraries of Fonts.com, MyFonts, Google Fonts, Membership by Monotype and Linotype. The fonts can be installed via SkyFonts™ and are thus available for all applications. At the end of the period for which the font has been purchased the font is automatically removed from the system. Time and experience will show which new models will emerge and be able to hold their ground in the long term next to the established providers. *(for more information see the chapter Providers and Licenses, p. 30)*

Currently, with HTML5[18] and CSS3[19] we have reached a point that is very promising for the future of web design and the use of fonts on the Web. Both are continuously developed further by the W3C, the World Wide Web Consortium[20]. For example, since the introduction of HTML5, the embedding of SVGs[21] has become standard and videos can be directly embedded, a process that used to require additional plug-ins, such as Flash. There is also better support for platforms and cross-system compatibility. However, there are some disadvantages as well. For example, not all innovations can currently be applied in all browsers. Yet the fact that all standard browsers are regularly updated with the latest versions considerably supports the establishment of new innovations on the Web in general and in the area of web fonts in particular. The web design scene is directly involved in many technical developments as the increased networking allows them to exchange information, discuss problems, and keep up to date with the latest developments.

We can therefore look forward to what the next few years are going to bring us and how technological developments will affect the handling of fonts on the Web.

Font Formats

For several decades the fonts that were available for use on the Web were limited to the ten so-called "core fonts" or "web safe fonts". They replaced the previous pixel fonts and improved the readability of web contents.

These fonts were pre-installed and activated as standard on almost all computers across all operating systems. They were designed specifically for on-screen text display. Microsoft optimized them during development in such a way that they are especially well rendered in small sizes between 9 and 16 pixels. Due to the limited pixels available for each character, this is a very complicated task. The process of adjusting a character to the pixel grid is called "hinting."

Even though in recent years a comprehensive technical change, the cloud-based external embedding of fonts on the Web, allowed the linking of other fonts from font foundries, the core fonts are still considered to be the best hinted fonts around – 13 years after their release for usage.

Overlap Web & Typography

Arial

Overlap Web & Typography

Georgia

Overlap Web & Typography

Verdana

Overlap Web & Typography

Impact

Overlap Web & Typography

Times New Roman

Overlap Web & Typography

Trebuchet MS

Overlap Web & Typography

Andale Mono

Overlap Web & Typography

Courier New

Overlap Web & Typography

Comic Sans MS

Webdings

fonts FOR screen?

Nowadays there are a great many fonts that can be embedded and used online. It seems as if core fonts are on their way out. In the past few years quite a few developments could be seen in terms of fonts found on the Web. Many developers discovered their love of experimentation and barrier-free readability is becoming a new focus.

Different font formats, browser-specific rasterizers, and individual hinting, nonetheless, still cause a large amount of confusion among newcomers to the application of fonts on the Web.

Which font format do I need and what is the difference among them?

How do I recognize a well-hinted font and what is hinting?

What providers are there and how do they differ from each other?

What type of license is best suited for my needs?

How does my font appear on various browsers?

PostScript

The PostScript font format was developed in 1982 by the Adobe founders Charles Geschke and John Warnock. The format replaced the raster-based bitmap fonts used at the time and made desktop publishing popular. It revolutionized the previous typesetting method (phototypesetting). The main difference to the previously used pixel fonts (bitmap fonts) was the fact that fonts were no longer drawn with the help of raster images but rather by cubic Bézier curves based on cubic equations. In the PostScript format the glyphs of every font are defined by PostScript operations. The outlines of the font's characters are stored and saved. The name of every glyph is connected with the associated outline definition within a dictionary.

Bitmap fonts

Currently, the PostScript format contains around ten different specifications. The most frequently used formats are the PostScript type 1 and type 3 format.

Type 3 is practically the predecessor of the type 1 format and its low budget version. Type 3 fonts do not have specified hinting, which can result in an unbalanced look of the fonts, especially in smaller sizes. Type 3 fonts are not supported by the Adobe Type Manager. Today this format specification is no longer in use.

The type 1 format is embedded in today's PostScript fonts. A limited excerpt of the entire PostScript language scope for describing glyphs is used in this case. The description is standardized by ISO 9541. This ISO standard defines the method with which

Third-degree Bézier curves

glyphs and collections of glyphs are named. Hints can only be defined in a standardized way among type 1 fonts. The hints determine the curves. The rasterizer can only receive hints about how the font is set up. The hints, however, only describe the horizontal and vertical scales of the font. These hints are then adopted by the rasterizer for all point sizes.

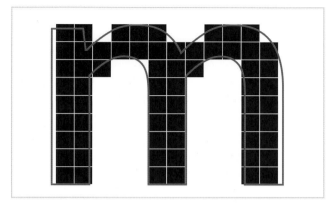

Hinting

Type 1 PostScript fonts are delivered in a package that contains at least two and generally four files.

.pfm (PostScript Font Metric) describes the character widths of the individual glyphs and kerning values for pairs of glyphs. It is only required for Windows.

.pfb (PostScript Font Binary) contains the information about the font as such. An equal variation of this format is the .pfa (PostScript Font ASCII). It contains only ASCII codes instead of an arbitrary number of bytes.

.inf (optional) is an ASCII text file, containing, for example, information about the dimensions of the characters or general encoding information. Similar to .pfm, this file format is only required for Windows.

.afm (Adobe Font Metrics, optional) is an optional alternative format for the .pfm file, containing the same information but in an easy to edit ASCII text format.

TrueType

The TrueType format was introduced for the first time in 1991 developed by Apple as an alternative to Adobe's PostScript format. Shortly thereafter, Microsoft also integrated the format into Windows (3.1). Apple passed on the license to Microsoft free of charge to increase its distribution range.

Similar to PostScript fonts, TrueType fonts are defined by outline vectors. In the TrueType font, these consist of quadratic B-splines. This means that these Bézier curves are calculated by quadratic equations. The older PostScript format by Adobe uses cubic Bézier curves instead.

Under windows, the font files are also called .ttf or .ttc, where ttc stands for TrueType Collection and describes collection files that contain several fonts. This type of collection files requires less storage space as the contained fonts share many TrueType tables.

In the TrueType format, the specification for how the rasterizer should handle the individual glyphs is not specified by hints as in the PostScript format, but by a set of instructions. They specify the curves for each individual glyph and can be affected by the specifications for the rasterizer.

The advantage of this procedure is that it can be specifically determined how the rasterizer should handle a point for every point size of the script. This way, all glyphs can be perfectly defined in all straight lines.

However, as specifying the instructions for every glyph of a font and font style is very elaborate, this advantage is used rather infrequently, which means that in practical application PostScript and TrueType formats do not differ much.

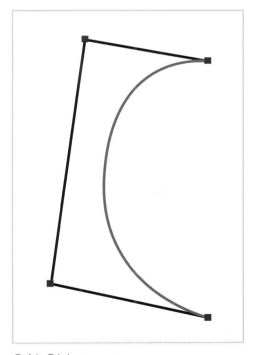

Cubic Bézier curves

OpenType

Initially developed by Microsoft alone and later in collaboration with Adobe, OpenType is a concept for a cross-system font format. Adobe and Microsoft decided to collaborate on the format to increase its user-friendliness and to create an environment for other joint innovations. It was first published in 1996. After the year 2000, a large number of fonts based on the OpenType format were introduced to the market.

The format incorporates the already existing TrueType and Adobe PostScript type 1 font formats. As an extension of the TrueType Open format by Microsoft, the OpenType format can contain either PostScript outlines (.otf), i.e. a curve description by quadratic splines, or TrueType contours (.ttf) that are described by cubic splines. It can be applied cross-platform and contains powerful, enhanced typographic functions based on the Unicode encoding standard. It thus accommodates alternative glyphs such as old-style figures, small caps, and swashes.

Quadratic B-splines

OpenType is compatible with all other current formats and can be used in conjunction with them in the same document. OpenType fonts are recognized and rendered on the screen by a PostScript raster program.

These raster programs are either installed as add-ons or are integrated into operating systems. OpenType supports the international Unicode encoding standard for extended language support and therefore contains enhanced fonts. Due to their compact data structure, the file sizes of OpenType fonts are comparatively small. The additional features that can be contained in OpenType fonts have only been applicable since CSS3 and HTML5 and so far are insufficiently supported by some browsers.

WOFF

Originally developed in 2009, the Web Open Font Format reappeared recently. An earlier version of the font format was not successful. It was created by the font developers Erik van Blokland and Tal Leming in cooperation with the Mozilla developer Jonathan Kew to improve the collaboration between font and browser developers. Similar to the OpenType format, it consists of a collection structure that can contain TrueType or OpenType fonts (PostScript fonts). The major advantage of the WOFF format is the fact that compressed data is directly stored in the file and the resulting file size reduction of 40% decreases the loading time on the Web.

A tool is embedded on the website for online decompression. Similar to most font formats, it is based on a SFNT structure (spline font) that contains tables of specifications such as the glyph outlines, horizontal metrics or font names. These tables exist independently of each other and can be complemented by additional tables that describe parts of the font. Tables that are required for specific programs or tools can also be added. The SFNT format was originally developed for Apple's TrueType fonts on Macintosh. It served as the basis of all other formats.

The WOFF format also supports the embedding of additional meta-information such as licensing information, information about the author, and the developer.

Currently, the format is supported by almost all current browsers and the W3C is already looking into the standardization of the WOFF 2.0. The latest Internet Explorer supports the WOFF format, while the older versions IE 4–8 still had to resort to the embedding of EOT files.

EOT

The abbreviation EOT stands for Embedded OpenType, which was developed by Microsoft for the Internet Explorer and has been in use since the late 1990s. It is a variation of the OpenType format and has the advantage that its compression makes it suitable for quick application on the Web. EOT fonts are also distinguished by the fact that they can be linked via URL to specific websites and thus only function on these websites that were previously specified by presetting. In the web font sector, EOT does not seem to have much of a future. While the latest Internet Explorer already supports the more convenient cross-browser WOFF format, the older versions of the Internet Explorer IE 4–8 could not utilize EOT fonts so far.

SVG

The Scalable Vector Graphics Format is a specification for the description of two-dimensional vector graphics. In 1998 two such specifications were submitted for standardization.

The Vector Markup Language (VML) by Microsoft and Macromedia as well as Precision Graphics Markup Language (PGML), which was developed by a cooperation of Adobe, IBM, Netscape and Sun. However, the W3C did not adopt either of the two languages but decided instead to combine them and develop them further. In September 2011 they were published under the name SVG 1.0. This recommendation was supported by most of the major players of the IT industry and accepted as the standard. Microsoft opposed this for a long time and until Internet Explorer 9 it did not support any SVG format fonts but used its own developed vector language VML. From Internet Explorer 10 they have abandoned this strategy and it no longer supports VMLs.

An upcoming format, SVG 2.0 is currently under development and is expected to be completed by 2016. It is supposed to contain some changes and improvements.

Fonts can be embedded in the respective SVG files. This is not recommended, however, as this would only consist of saved outlines of the glyphs that are displayed on the drawing surface of the SVG graphic. For a short period of time, the SVG format was of interest in the web font sector as it could be used in some browser versions that do not support any other web font formats.

Some providers still offer fonts in the SVG format. These are no longer relevant to professional web font application.

Nevertheless, SVG is experiencing a minor comeback currently as it allows the simple and reliable creation of flexibly applicable icon fonts. The advantage of inline SVG-based fonts is the fact that in modern browsers the contents can be directly integrated into HTML. Among other features, this allows access to and modification of the elements via CSS and JavaScript. Other advantages of inline SVG icons include the fact that they can be better positioned and multi-colored and also offer special effects such as blur filters.

Icon fonts

Icon fonts, such as dingbats, were formerly used to insert scalable icons. However, they have some problems when used on the Web. They can only be used monochrome and it is difficult to control their positioning as, similar to a font, they are reliant on line height, vertical alignment, letter spacing and word spacing.

The fact that icon fonts are treated like fonts can also be seen in the rendering. Anti-aliasing may cause the actually quite sharp graphics to appear rather blurred. In addition, their loading time leaves much to be desired as they are usually only shown with a delay.

In recent times, however, in the area of web fonts when it comes to icon fonts or pictogram depiction, inline SVGs are increasingly applied. Due to some new features that were introduced with HTML 5, icon fonts are currently experiencing a renaissance.

A good example for a widely used icon font is the Font Awesome a free font that can be used for every icon you will need on your website.

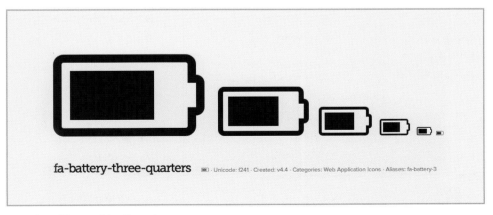

Icon font "Battery" by Font Awesome

Web Application Icons

◐ adjust	⚓ anchor	▣ archive
✛ arrows	↔ arrows-h	↕ arrows-v
@ at	🚗 automobile (alias)	⚖ balance-scale
🏛 bank (alias)	📊 bar-chart	📊 bar-chart-o (alias)
≡ bars	▭ battery-0 (alias)	▭ battery-1 (alias)
▣ battery-3 (alias)	▣ battery-4 (alias)	▭ battery-empty
▣ battery-half	▣ battery-quarter	▣ battery-three-quarters
🍺 beer	🔔 bell	🔔 bell-o
bell-slash-o	🚲 bicycle	binoculars
⚡ bolt	💣 bomb	📗 book
🔖 bookmark-o	💼 briefcase	bug
🏢 building-o	📢 bullhorn	◎ bullseye

66 New Icons in 4.4

5oo 500px	a amazon	⚖ balance-scale
▣ battery-1 (alias)	▣ battery-2 (alias)	▣ battery-3 (alias)
▭ battery-empty	▣ battery-full	▣ battery-half
▣ battery-three-quarters	black-tie	calendar-check-o
calendar-plus-o	calendar-times-o	cc-diners-club
chrome	clone	💬 commenting
contao	creative-commons	expeditedssl
fonticons	○ genderless	get-pocket
gg-circle	hand-grab-o (alias)	hand-lizard-o
hand-peace-o	hand-pointer-o	hand-rock-o
hand-spock-o	hand-stop-o (alias)	⌛ hourglass

List of icon fonts at www.fontawesome.de

Hinting, Anti-aliasing and Rasterizers

To understand the processes of hinting and anti-aliasing for the optimization of modern vector-based fonts for on-screen use, we should first have a look at the earliest digital fonts.

To comply with the low resolution of screens at the time, these fonts, which were known as bitmap fonts, had to be created as arrays of pixel matrixes. As a mere 8x8 pixels were available for each character (for example in the Commodore C-64 with a screen resolution of 320x200 pixels), majuscules were almost exclusively used for the depiction of fonts and even these had to be manually adjusted to the grid. Minuscules would have only caused problems in such a grid and were virtually never used.

These first bitmap fonts were not scalable and therefore distinguishing headlines from body copy, for example, was only possible by using a different style of the font or even another font that was designed at a larger scale. Bitmap fonts therefore have a major disadvantage that they are quite tedious to handle – optimizing and adjusting a font to a raster of a certain size had to be done separately for each set.

Web design of the 1990s was dominated by this type of fonts. This is unthinkable today as the introduction of vector-based fonts gives us much more variables to work with.

As we all know, the screens of digital devices still consist of pixels, but most fonts today are based on vectors. A screen is therefore not capable of depicting vectors, which are not defined by pixel matrixes but instead consist of mathematically defined curves and lines.

As a result, the computer is forced to convert the vectors into a pixel matrix via software. The so-called rasterizer, however, is faced by another problem: when rasterizing the font it cannot employ pure mathematics and treat every font the same way. A computer has a number of raster options with which it can convert a font.

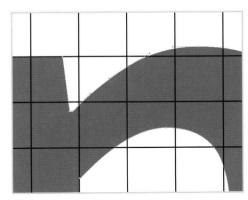

Bézier curves on rasters

With the 1-bit method black pixels are displayed on a white background. There are no gradations. The matrix consists of purely YES/NO options. The computer decides with a simple calculation whether the pixel is shown in black or white. Looking at a square of a raster in which the vector is located, the computer decides on YES (i.e. the depiction of a fully black pixel) if more than 50% of a square is covered by the vector. Most fonts are not really optimally displayed this way. Often the font is displayed with a completely different effect and does not resemble the original 100%. This does not include fonts that were specifically optimized for this purpose.

1-bit method

The so-called gray-scale smoothing, also known as anti-aliasing is less rigorous when displaying a font. The underlying principle is the same as for the 1-bit method, but the computer no longer only has the options of yes and no, but rather has a number of gradations. The more of the square's surface is covered by the vector, the darker it is displayed. The opposite, of course also applies: the less the surface is covered the less the black content of the pixels. The problem with this method is that the font often appears blurred in small sizes. To the eye, the high gray content around the pixel resembles the blurring effect in Photoshop. This is only a problem when rendering small sizes on low resolution screens. The larger the font or the higher the resolution of the end device, the less problems occur with this technique. It enlarges the pixel raster of the font and ensures that our eye sees less of the gray, making the font appear sharper.

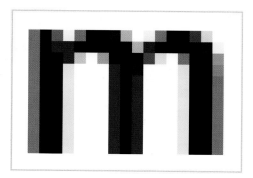

Grayscale smoothing/anti-aliasing

The final, and currently most interesting option for rasterization is subpixel rendering, a special form of anti-aliasing. Almost all modern LCD monitors have a pixel resolution, in which the individual pixels are divided into three subpixel strips.

The RGB subpixels (green, blue, red, from left to right) allow even finer smoothing of fonts. If a pixel is rendered in gray as in grayscale rendering, then all colors are equally active and bright. However, if the pixel is illuminated in red then the focus of the intensity is visually shifted to the left. If a pixel is illuminated in green, then the same effect occurs to the right. The observer does not see this coloration of the pixels as it is too far away from the eye to recognize. However, it considerably affects the readability of the font, which appears sharper as this method triples the horizontal resolution of the font.

Subpixel rendering is not yet used on mobile output devices, as these can be turned in four different directions. To implement subpixel rendering, four different rendering preset values would be required that would not allow uniform rendering of the font. It remains to be seen whether this effect will continue to be required by screens with improved resolutions in the future. One thing is for sure, though, the rasterizer system developed by software manufacturers has substantially contributed to the advancement of handling typography on screens and especially to the rendering of vector-based fonts.

Due to the many interference factors and different requirements there will not be the ONE solution (yet).

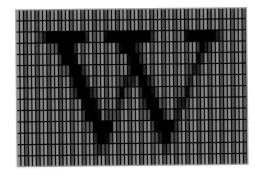

RGB subpixel rendering

The rendering of a font not only depends on the applied operating system, but also on the browser of the user or the font format.

The files of most professional web fonts contain additional digital information that provides instructions of how the font should be rendered on the raster. This allows the control of the optimal readability of a font in smaller sizes or with lower resolutions. This information is known as hinting. Fonts can be automatically or manually hinted. Hints generated by font editors such as Fontographer or Fontlab are frequently used since manual hinting is extremely time consuming. In contrast to manual hints, automatic hints are not individually configured for each glyph, but there is nothing to be said against using them. In most cases, manual font hinting is an indication of the high quality of the web font in general, it can be seen that even with manually hinted fonts there is some loss of typographic characteristics, especially in smaller sizes.

Even if the underlying information is embedded in the applied font format, most operating systems have their own rasterizers and thus in some instances fonts that were optimized for a specific process are not optimally rendered on some operating systems. The system ignores the information included in the font file and applies its own process. Almost all font foundries therefore offer various versions of the same font formats. They differ in the hinting information to comply with different browsers. Depending on the requirements, a different format is delivered.

To better understand this problem, one should take a closer look at the different rendering engines of Microsoft and Apple.

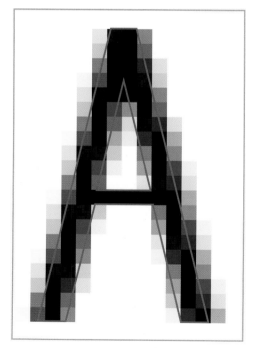

Hinting of the "A" of Open Sans compared to vector rendering

Rendering Engines and Browsers

It seems that the different providers have different convictions of which rasterizer systems offer the best possible results when hinting a font.

To date, all windows systems use GDI/GDI+-API for ClearType rendering. ClearType rendering is a mix between subpixel rendering and the 1-bit method. For large font sizes in particular, this is problematic because ClearType provides only horizontal, not vertical rendering and does not render curves. This causes unattractive saw-tooth edges, especially in larger font sizes. This problem is not resolved even with well-hinted fonts. ClearType rendering under Windows basically attempts to fit as many glyph sections as possible to the pixel grid. Consequently, especially the stems of a font are rendered one pixel wide where possible, which often causes them to lose their particular appearance.

With Internet Explorer 9, DirectWrite was introduced. As opposed to GDI/GDI+, DirectWrite also supports vertical edge smoothing while ensuring that the individual glyphs are given the proper spacing. Currently, Windows Chrome (version 16) still uses GDI rendering, while Firefox from version 4 upwards and Internet Explorer from version 9 upwards already support DirectWrite. This primarily accelerates font rendering. Thanks to DirectWrite it has become possible to render @font-face fonts for the first time in Firefox.

Nevertheless, users must manually activate it. GDI rasterizers supported by DirectWrite then ensure that the fonts can increasingly also be fitted on subpixels and thus smoothly scaled. Even in special situations like if the screen is turned, the font remains remarkably clear. At the same time, the gray-scale smoothing on older browser versions also renders hinted TrueType fonts surprisingly well. With the former gray-scale smoothing by Windows, unhinted fonts looked rather good and were relatively well-matched to the raster by the ClearType system, yet this often resulted in unattractive saw-tooth edges and stems with varying weights. This once again proves that unhinted fonts are not an option. PostScript fonts are always rendered by Windows with gray-scale smoothing as it does not support subpixel rendering. In due time, DirectWrite will probably replace the current windows rendering systems.

Under iOS and OS X, the Quartz multitool is used, or rather not used, as Quartz ignores all preset hinting rules of a font. Therefore PostScript and TrueType fonts are rendered in the same way, even though the available hinting for TrueType fonts constitutes the big difference between the two formats. In iOS and OS

Font "Aller", unhinted under Chrome

X, Quartz handles the rasterizing of TrueType, OpenType and PostScript-based fonts, but also the depiction of graphics in PDF documents. Apple focuses on not deforming a font to match the pixel raster, which is essentially not a bad idea. However, this makes fonts sometimes look heavier than they really are while also appearing blurred. This is rather annoying to many Windows users. There is not much to say about different browsers and their rasterizers under iOS and OS X, as Quartz is the exclusive tool used for rasterization.

Many designers are currently bothered by the fact that they have no control over rendering under iOS and OS X. Nevertheless, it is important to select well-hinted fonts to meet the needs of all users. Perhaps the rendering systems of the two large providers will be synchronized, at least in terms of technology. For designers this would offer the advantage of not having to spend a lot of time testing a font on all devices of various manufacturers and browsers to ensure that it is legible enough throughout. In addition, there would be fewer problems in chosing a font format, as True-Type fonts in particular whose embedded hints include the rendering information of a font, have a lot of possibilities. It would be desirable for all involved if these could be fully used.

meine Copy, gebt mei
Body nochn Durchsch

Open Sans (TT) under Chrome with DirectWrite

Copy, gebt meinem E
nochn Durchschuss!

Open Sans (TT) under Chrome without DirectWrite

einem üblen Geviert ta
sie des Grauwerts anbl

Open Sans (TT) under IE9 with DirectWrite

Providers and Licenses

As the selection of available fonts increased, the number of font providers also mushroomed. Users should carefully check their background, however, and for professional use it is better to rely on the large and established font vendors.

To date, not all print typefaces are available with web font licenses, not to mention special optimization for on-screen use. For this reason, almost all large and small font foundries are constantly working on licensing a majority of their font libraries for web use.

Licensing models tailored to the specific use and user needs are currently in the experimentation phase. It is also possible that new licensing models will emerge in which the focus is on the volume of use. Currently, for print typeface licenses the same costs are charged regardless of whether they are used for many years by a large agency or if a freelance graphic designer uses a font a single time for a corporate identity. In the web sector, licensing is handled differently. For cloud-based font licenses, the volume of usage can be found in the server statistics to determine, for example, the "clicks per month/year". For self-hosting there is the option of embedding a count pixel or the license and its payment are based on permanent use.

Most of the key players on the market have opted for licenses based on "click per month", but also offer usage-based affordable and attractive offers. However, one can but wonder about some price models, for example when it comes to using fonts in apps, in particular for offline or similar concepts, an individual offer needs to be obtained, which drives the price up.

Therefore, potential buyers should consider some tactical and technical issues before buying font licenses. Do I pay for a font that is with a one-time license payment or with a monthly or yearly subscription? Do I buy the license for an individual font style, a font family or an entire collection or catalog? Are raw fonts included that I can use for web layout tests or do I only get a cloud-based embedding code? Is a free of charge font an alternative for me? Self-hosting offers the advantage that all technical matters are controllable. This prevents unwanted updates or a crashing of the cloud service. In return, with cloud hosting there are no worries about the technical embedding, upcoming browser changes and the subsequent adjustment, or the delivery speed.

Some providers also offer subscriptions that include a large range of fonts that are then freely available for individual use in every project. However, it is important to note that most providers do not allow the use of a purchased or leased font on several customer websites. Unfortunately, in such cases the website operators, i.e. the customers, must purchase the license themselves. It is relatively easy to find out which fonts and license models are required for which customer. A large company with a distinguished font that has been in use for many years and that works well on the Web and is available for web use would be well advised to invest the money in the license for the font. While the advantages and disadvantages of changing a font of a corporate identity is possibly self-explanatory for designers, convincing a customer of this is sometimes difficult, but not impossible. Students who are creating their own portfolios, on the other hand, can resort to one of the freely available good web fonts without hesitation.

To test the favored font up ahead, many providers offer free of charge developer accounts. Just sign up and test the font for a few days. After the trial period, the cloud-based embedding expires and the font is automatically replaced by a back up system font. This allows users to take their time to decide on a font or the required license model.

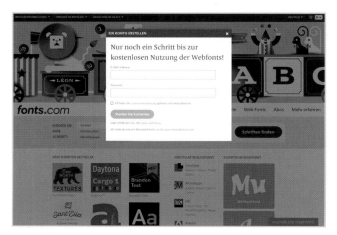

Screenshot: free of charge developer account www.fonts.com

MyFonts

Together with Fonts.com and Linotype, MyFonts belongs to the Monotype Inc. corporation, which has a history of being one of the leading providers of products and services in the typography sector since the 19th century. The mission of MyFonts as stated on the company's website is "to make it simple for everyone to find and buy fonts." To this end, MyFonts is constantly developing new tools, such as WhatTheFont, which allows users to upload the image of a font to be told what font it is and to find it faster. It is not difficult to find one's way around the font library of MyFonts. Various categorizations facilitate the search for a font or font category. The offer is subdivided into fonts, web fonts, foundries, best sellers, hot new fonts and special offers, as well as tags that aid the categorization of every font. Categories include display, headline, poster, branding, alternates, handmade, casual, and many more.

The library of MyFonts contains all current fonts and font families of the established font foundries. At the same time, fonts by rather less well-known font designers can also be purchased here, as MyFonts offers them a platform where they can conveniently market their fonts and receive a fair share of the profits. The selection of fonts at MyFonts includes 14,000 web fonts for self-hosting. There is also the option of testing a font for 30 days free of charge on one's own website before buying. Web font licenses at MyFonts are paid only once. There are no subscriptions but payment is based on an expected page views model. The font can then by used on several websites. If, due to multiple embedding the "clicks per month" rate exceeds the paid page views license model, the buyer can expand the license by purchasing additional page views. The purchase includes a web font kit for download that facilitates self-hosting. It already contains CSS (or Java) information.

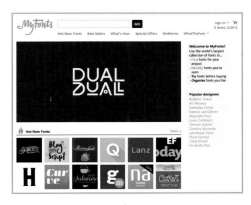

Screenshot www.myfonts.com

Fonts.com

Another company belonging to Monotype Inc., in addition to MyFonts and Linotype, Fonts.com offers more than 150,000 fonts for licensing, including around 10,000 web fonts, making it one of the best-equipped web font libraries. In addition, Fonts.com offers a collection of fonts that were carefully manually optimized for on-screen use as well as optimal support of OpenType functions even for older browsers.

As opposed to MyFonts, Fonts.com is a subscription service. Similar to MyFonts, fonts can also be licensed individually. However, a subscription is worthwhile to benefit from the entire product range. At Fonts.com the licensing models are based on a page views model. Free of charge use is available for less than 25,000 clicks. If this number is exceeded, a subscription is required. From 1,000,000 page views, a pro account is required, which is available for a rather modest amount of € 38.00 per month. With this pro account the web fonts can also be implemented on a more individual basis. User are given the option of either embedding them via the well-developed global server network of Fonts.com or host the fonts themselves.

The associated web design tool Typecast can only be fully utilized from a pro account. *(for more information see the chapter Technology, p. 92ff)*

Mock up or desktop fonts for testing a font within a project can be used with a free of charge account via SkyFonts™ for 24 hours in combination with the standard CS programs, while the web font preview allows the testing of fonts on websites by entering the URL.

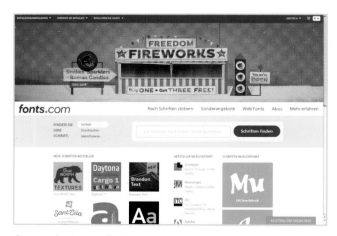

Screenshot www.fonts.com

Linotype

Since 2006, the long-standing company of Bad Homburg, Germany belongs to Monotype Inc. together with Fonts.com and MyFonts. With a history going back 125 years already, Linotype has evolved into one of the most important font libraries worldwide. Even the well-known Linotype FontExplorer as a program for font management was developed by Linotype and is today a part of everyday typographic use.

At Linotype, licenses for individual web fonts or entire font families are not acquired by subscription. Following a free of charge registration, the suitable page views model can be selected and the font acquired with a one-time payment. The use of the purchased page views has no time limit. If the "clicks-per-month" rate is exceeded, an additional license must be purchased. The desktop font version of the web font can be purchased along with the web font at half the price. After purchasing the font, the buyer receives a web font kit, as Linotype only offers self-hosting. The fonts at Linotype are divided according to typographic categories or application areas, which facilitates searching the library.

Screenshot www.linotype.com

FontShop

In addition to the marketing of fonts, Font-Shop is also specialized in the development of individual corporate fonts. FontShop developed corporate fonts for customers such as Süddeutsche Zeitung, dm-Drogeriemarkt, SAT.1, and Fritz-Kola. FontShop always focuses on the optimization of the developed font for digital use. Its Webfonter tool allows the free of charge testing of fonts on any website without registration, similar to the web font previewer tool of all providers belonging to Monotype.Inc. In addition, FontShop developed a plug-in for Photoshop that allows all graphic designers and web developers to test their projects with all FontShop fonts and to present them to their customers before buying the font.

At FontShop, fonts can be purchased individually or as sets. The web kit includes comp fonts that can be used for design purposes. The license of the font has no time limitation and, similar to most providers, the price is based on the monthly page views model of all websites on which the font is used. Currently, the fonts purchased for self-hosting can unfortunately only be used with Internet Explorer and Firefox. To ensure that all users see the fonts properly, there is the option of hosting the fonts free of charge via Typekit.

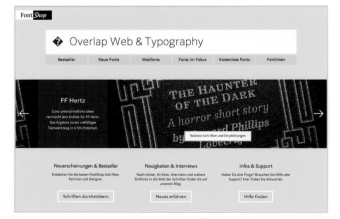

Screenshot www.fontshop.com

Adobe Typekit

Purchased in 2011 by Adobe, Typekit was originally founded in 2008 by some developers and graphic designers with the aim of marketing high-quality fonts independent of the large font foundries. Among others, Typekit offers fonts by Exljbris along with some classic fonts.

The Typekit library is very user-friendly. A clearly-structured side bar provides selection options such as classification, availability for web use, or application options such as headlines or body text.

Typekit offers classic fonts such as JAF Facit, FF Tisa and Brandon. After many years of improvements, Typekit has expanded its web font support to better incorporate Chinese, Japanese and Korean fonts. With its so-called "dynamic kit", which is included with the font, the very large and extensive East Asian fonts can be individually compressed with an option called "dynamic subsetting," with which essentially only those glyphs of a font are activated that are in use. This reduces the loading time of the often unmanageably large fonts.

Typekit offers web fonts exclusively via subscription, which requires a registration at Adobe that can be canceled at any time. The portfolio rate is around $ 50 per year and pays off mainly for web designers and graphic designers who work on a large number of projects. This subscription offers unlimited access to the entire library of Typekit with more that 1000 fonts and the simultaneous use of up to 100 fonts in various projects.

However, the page views number of Typekit's portfolio rate is limited to 500,000 per month. For smaller projects there is a free of charge test rate with which users can select two fonts from just above 130 fonts to use on a website as long as the number of page views does not exceed 25,000.

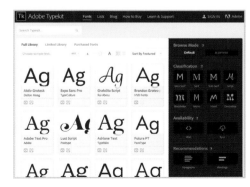

Screenshot www.typekit.com

Adobe Edge Web Fonts

After the takeover by Typekit in 2011, Adobe Edge Web Fonts has been marketing the web fonts of Adobe System as well as some Google fonts based on the collaboration between the two companies. This is why Adobe Edge Web Fonts offers more than 500 open-source font families free of charge without subscription. The simple search function for font selection resembles that of Typekit. Search filters allow classification according to serif, sans-serif and monospace fonts, while additional properties such as x-height and tracking can be entered, which is an advantage when selecting fonts for use on the Web. As all web fonts are available free of charge, it is no problem to install several fonts at the same time on a website or to use a single font on several websites. However, Adobe Edge Web Fonts does not offer self-hosting. As the fonts are provided via Typekit, quick loading and stability are ensured.

Google Fonts

With Google Fonts, Google Inc. possibly offers the largest open-source font library around. As the focus is on free of charge use, it does not contain fonts by well-known vendors. The more than 600 fonts were for the most part created by unknown designers, and can be adjusted and optimized anytime with their open-source license. Google Fonts even explicitly welcomes the contribution of anyone who is interested in optimizing the fonts. Similar to Adobe Edge, the number of fonts that can be integrated on a website is unlimited. When downloading the fonts it is possble to receive a package of several fonts for a website including the respective CSS and JavaScript code. To prevent long loading times of the fonts on the website, the package for a particular page should only contain the fonts that are actually used there. As opposed to Adobe Edge Web Fonts, the fonts of the Google Fonts library can also be downloaded for desktop use.

FontSquirrel

Similar to Adobe Edge Web Fonts and Google Fonts, FontSquirrel also provides handpicked web fonts free of charge. FontSquirrel is a cooperation partner of the US font license distributor FontSpring, offering more than 800 font families by foundries such as Ascender Fonts and Exljbris. Fonts are also divided according to classifications and tags. They include fonts such as Source Sans Pro or Fira Sans, which are also found at Google Fonts and Adobe Edge Web Fonts, as well as interesting, unusual, hand-picked fonts such as Pacifico or Lobster. FontSquirrel does not offer third-party hosting services. The fonts are only available for download for self-hosting. If one of the offered fonts is not available as a web font kit for download, FontSquirrel offers a special free of charge service, the Webfont Generator. With the required authorization it can be used to upload desktop fonts and create web font kits from them. FontSquirrel trusts the users not to generate web font kits from fonts that do not have the corresponding license. There are three upload options available: Basic, Optimal and Expert. In the expert mode, even settings such as rendering options or font formats can be determined and the subsetting adjusted. This reduces loading times, for example. When it comes to carefully selected, free of charge web fonts, FontSquirrel is a viable alternative to Google Fonts for those who prefer self-hosting.

Screenshot www.Fontsquirrel.de

Webtype

Webtype offers a web font library with more than 120 font families, including classic fonts such as Gill Sans®, Calibri, or Garamond. Licenses are only available as yearly subscriptions. Similar to most providers, the payment varies according to the page views model. At the same time, Webtype also offers a user-friendly payment model with tolerances – if the page views number is exceeded, an additional license must only be purchased if the number of visitors exceeds 20%. In addition, similar to MyFonts, a font can be tested for 30 days free of charge prior to purchasing the license. As a rule, the purchased fonts are third-party hosted via Webtype by embedding a CSS code. Self-hosting is possible, but only from an annual payment of $400, with monthly page views at a high rate of up to 12.5 million views.

Similar to Fonts.com, Webtype offers a tool for testing fonts on websites. The so-called FontSwapper can be used without a registration, but unlike the WebFontsPreview of Fonts.com, it does not offer the option of displaying the CSS code.

Screenshot www.webtype.com

Providers Compared

Provider	Range of Fonts	Publishing Options
MyFonts	More than 23,000 web fonts	CSS, self-hosting available
Fonts.com	More than 10,000 web fonts	CSS or JavaScript, self-hosting available from PRO package
Linotype	More than 150 web fonts	CSS or JavaScript, self-hosting available
FontShop	More than 3,000 web fonts	CSS or JavaScript, self-hosting available
Adobe Typekit	More than 1,000 web fonts	JavaScript, self-hosting NOT available
Adobe Edge Web Fonts	More than 500 web fonts	JavaScript, self-hosting NOT available
Google Fonts	More than 600 web fonts	CSS, self-hosting available
FontSquirrel	More than 800 fonts (approx. 50 web fonts + web font generator)	CSS, self-hosting available
Webtype	More than 100 web fonts	CSS, self-hosting from LARGE package available

Payment Interval	Desktop Use	Tools
One-time payment based on the expected monthly page views	Desktop license required	Typecast, WhatTheFont
Monthly, annually, or every three years	Only from annual payment and for pro and master packages	SkyFonts™, WebFontsPreview.com, Fonts.com Webfonts extension for PS
Payment, renewed payment after page views have been used up	Desktop license required	–
One-time payment	Desktop license required	Plug-ins for Photoshop, Illustrator, InDesign and Fireworks, WebFonter
Annually	Available as part of the Creative Cloud subscription	Adobe Creative Cloud, Browser Samples, Type Tester
Free of charge	Not available	–
Free of charge	Yes, available unlimited and free of charge	Font Previewer
Free of charge	Yes, available unlimited and free of charge	Webfont Generator
Annually	Not available	FontSwapper

Unconventional Providers

SkyFonts™

SkyFonts™ is a system developed by Monotype offering a new licensing model. Initially introduced as an independent product, Monotype has in the meantime incorporated SkyFonts™ with the providers belonging to the company.

SkyFonts™ offers a lightweight program or a download app, which runs in the background on the PC and allows the use of the fonts of all providers belonging to Monotype Inc. for desktop use. The desired font is selected via SkyFonts™ and then activated for a specific amount of time on all standard desktop programs. The combination of Fonts.com, MyFonts, Linotype, and Google Fonts offers a huge selection of thousands of high-quality fonts.

The offered licenses range from a free test account to a master subscription level. With the free account the web fonts can be tested for five minutes on the user's workstation. With the intermediate licensing model, the professional level, five fonts can be activated on the user's desktop for a duration of 30 days, coupled with access to around 20,000 web fonts, as well as the option of managing the fonts via the FontExplorer X. At the master subscription level there are no more limitations . For around € 89, all fonts can be used on the user's workstation without limitation, including all web fonts. If the duration of the license expires, SkyFonts™ removes the font from the system so that it is no longer available for use on the desktop. The concept is particularly interesting for designers who like to test various fonts for an extended period of time before actually purchasing them. However, opinions vary about the usefulness of a test period of five minutes as this is definitely not enough time for any serious testing.

Fontstand

Fontstand was introduced for the first time in 2015 and, similar to SkyFonts™, it is a service that allows the testing of fonts on one's own desktop applications for a specific period of time you can choose.

The system for licensing fonts of various independent labels was conceived by font designers, including Peter Bil'ak (Typotheque), and includes the fonts of around 24 different small foundries such as Fontsmith, Typejockeys, House Industries, TypeTogether, and many others.

Upon registration, users have the opportunity of testing a font free of charge for one hour. If they want to continue using the font, they can lease it on a monthly basis for 10% of the entire cost of the font. After the font has been leased for 12 months, the license is tranferred into a desktop license and is considered paid off. Fontstand is therefore a system that can be recommended as it offers a new type of model with very fair conditions.

Currently, the app for download for the desktop is only available for Mac OS X. A version to include Windows is already under development.

Similar to most providers, once the app is installed the fonts can be selected according to categories. As opposed to other providers, however, Fontstand does not offer forced permanent leasing solutions and the fact that it primarily offers fonts that are rarely found at the large providers such as Monotype render the service even more interesting for users who value high-quality individual fonts.

Unfortunately, so far Fontstand provides desktop license exclusively, as not all fonts are available with a web license and those that are cannot be purchased from Fontstand but must instead be directly requested and purchased from the respective font foundry. These offer primarily self-hosting solutions that are available for a fixed one-time payment.

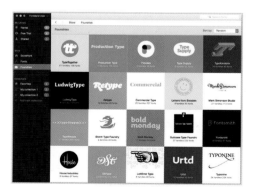

Screenshot www.fontstand.com

Selecting a Font

Similar to print typography, there are also a number of on-screen typography rules and regulations to be observed. Contrary to print, however, where books by well-known typographers have been published regularly for nearly 100 years, in the web typography sector there are few solid sources that designers can rely on.

The greatest amount of knowledge in this area is distributed across many blogs and Internet pages that constantly contradict each other all the time or offer a quick course in print typography, occasionally even limiting themselves to this as they are generally written by programmers for programmers. The most prominent problem is that designers have to take different screen sizes into account and at the same time the screen resolutions were never as varied as they are today. The same font can look differently on various screens, which often complicates the practical application of a chosen font.

The following small, self-tested list of guidelines presents an overview of the most important rules and some reference points for identifying fonts that can be used without hesitation on the Web.

Methods with which the fonts of headlines and body copy can be optimized to increase readability also play an important role in this aspect. In addition to project-specific criteria with which the designers decide for themselves which font is suitable for the project at hand, there are a few other criteria to observe on the Web. For example, the type of media, such as mobile phones or tabs on which the font is expected to work and how much text is included in the projects. If there is a clear focus on long texts, then the font should be chosen carefully and deliberately and much thought be given to which font is the most suitable and meets all requirements. If the focus is mostly on images and the text is purely informative with short segments, then the choice is a little easier. In general, the advantages and disadvantages of an individual font or of two fonts compared to each other should be very closely examined.

Given the constantly evolving technology and the large number of fonts that are published daily, most of these rules are not carved in stone and should be treated as recommendations. This is precisely what makes web typography so fascinating. Practically any day a new idea could revolutionize the whole sector.

"As more typefaces hit the scene, we need to understand how they can best serve our designs, and to push ourselves to move beyond more novelty in our selections. If much of the web is made up of text – and it is – web typography can be a very powerful tool indeed."

Jason Santa Maria (Creative Director, Typekit)

What makes a font suitable for use on screens? Following are some features that define a font that can be used without hesitation on the screen.

Slightly elevated x-height

Since in small sizes in particular only limited pixels are available to create the shape of the glyph, every pixel counts. An elevated x-height considerably facilitates depiction as the individual parts of the glyph, such as the stem or counters, are given more space on the pixel raster and therefore there are more pixels available to present them in a clearer way.

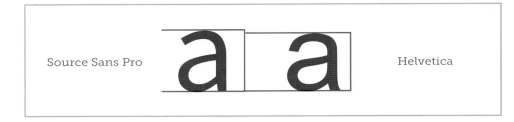

Source Sans Pro   Helvetica

Slightly open counters

The shape of the characters is almost as important as an elevated x-height. To appear larger, many fonts that are successful on the Web feature slightly open white space inside the characters (open counters). In practical terms this means that in lowercase letters such as the small "e" the open counter (the lower curve) is rather open, unlike Helvetica, where the curve almost touches the top eye. The same applies to closed counters. The larger they are, the easier it is to depict the shape of the character as the pixels interfere less with each other.

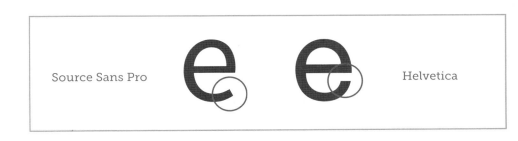

Source Sans Pro   Helvetica

Distinctive stroke weight differences

Again, the geometric pixel raster limits our font choice. Currently, fonts with distinctive stroke weight contrasts can be depicted, and it is therefore not necessary to create a million websites with the same Grotesque font. However, care should be taken that there are clear contrasts as slight stroke weight variations may not be depicted properly on some screens. The thinnest hairline should also not be too thin, as in the case of a Bodoni font. Open counters should also be kept in mind when choosing a font according to this criterion.

Source Sans Pro   a a   Bodoni

Increased tracking

It seems as if there is no end to the topic of openness in typographical web design, as tracking should also be slightly increased for web fonts (attention: not all browsers master subpixels at this time). This is because the black/white contrast is more intense on screen than in print and as a result black areas appear darker and tend to blend into each other.

Hamburgefonts

Hamburgefonts

Serif or sans serif, that is the question

There are some design conventions that were established through the years and that continue to be difficult to resist. In the print sector, the rule that magazines should be exclusively printed with serif fonts has dissolved over the years. There are very few areas where only either serif or sans-serif fonts are "allowed." This level has not been reached on the Web. Since in the early days of the Internet, screens had very low resolutions, for a long time the rule of thumb of no serif on the screen was applied. This was because in the wide-meshed pixel raster, the fine serifs were barely visible while the larger serifs usually appeared too bulky and too wide. However, due to the numerous technical improvements since that time our current operating systems, browsers, font files and of course hardware generally have no problems depicting serif fonts anymore. Only in very small sizes one has to be a bit careful with serif fonts. Nowadays there are even fonts that have been optimized for this purpose such as the Reading Edge™ Series by Font Bureau.

Serif **Headline**

Nein, meine Texte les ich nicht, so nicht, stöhnte Oxmox. Er war mit Franklin, Rockwell und dem halbtaxgrauen Panther Weidemann in Memphis (Heartbreak Hotel) zugange. Sie warteten auf die fette Gill, um bei der Bank of Helvetica die Kapitälchen in Kapital umzuwandeln. Oxmox liess nicht locker. Ich fleh euch an, rettet meine Copy, gebt meinem Body nochn Durchschuss! Kein Problem, erbarmte sich Old Face Baskerville, streichelte seinen Hund, zog seine einspaltige Poppl, legte an und traf! (Zeidank nichts Ernstes nurn bisschen Fraktur.) Oxmox: Danke, ist jetzt mit

Example combination of serif and sans-serif fonts

Line length

In print there is a rule of thumb that for copy text the line length should be around 70 characters. On the Internet it is not easy to ensure that the lines are displayed at the same length for
all users. However, a line length from 70 to 90 characters is a good basis for comfortable reading. If there are less characters per line the layout becomes very uneven due to the incomplete
or missing hyphenation. With longer lines it becomes difficult to return to the beginning of the
line. What is more, if the line length is not precisely specified in the CSS, it is possible that in
cinemas or other large screens the lines can run right to edge, which in the worst case scena-
rio is defined by pixels. Depending on the display, this can result in line lengths of up to 50 cm
or more. We know from print typography that such lines are not suitable for reading large
amounts of text.

Line spacing

When it comes to the optimal line spacing, the number of approaches and opinions found on
the Internet can be very confusing. Standard line spacing is pre-set by every browser as standard but can also be adjusted by the user by changing the default setting. It is important that it is
defined by values such as "EM", "percent", etc. When using pixel information for font sizes and
line spacing, the user settings are overwritten. As a result, when zooming on a website, the
values remain constant and have no chance of adjustment. EM and percentage, on the other
hand adjust to the browser of the end user. The major recommendation for spacing is: more
room! As mentioned above for the choice of fonts, web fonts require more space than fonts of
the print sector. Therefore it is better to select slightly wider line spacing. As a rule, the longer
the lines the wider the line spacing. A good minimum value is double the cap height. Based on
the used font, line length, font size, etc. this value can even be slightly increased. For smaller
sizes in particular, too little line spacing can be problematic. For larger font sizes (from around
20 px), the line spacing can be reduced.

Finding the right font is not everything. Similar to print, there are a number of other factors that must be taken into account when aiming at good typography.

Font size

An absolute minimum font size of 9px is probably commendable. On the one hand, fonts that are smaller than this are difficult to read; on the other hand an "x" requires at least five pixels of height to depict. The 9px are not applicable to all fonts, but are rather the exception. For example, the Reading Edge™ Series by Font Bureau has been especially optimized for reading in small sizes, i.e. text sizes between 9 to 18px. With fonts that have not been optimized for this purpose, this size can quickly become uncomfortable. Instead, a standard size of 14px is recommended. However, in previous years there is a growing trend on the Web to provide enough room for everything, including fonts. Thus there is an increase of reading texts sized 18px and more. In this case it is probably up to designers to find the suitable font for their applications and their specific styles. As already stated for line spacing, it is best not to provide pixel information, but to define page via EMs and percentages.

Reading Edge™ Series

Font Bureau developed ten fonts that were especially designed and optimized for small sizes on screen. They have adjusted x-heights and stroke weights to prevent the loss of details in small sizes. This results in lower contrast that ensures a balanced display. The typefaces were also developed with naturally wider and open glyph shapes. These factors render the ten fonts optimally readable, even in smallest sizes of 9px and less.

They can be found at: www.Font Bureau.com/ReadingEdge

Left:
Reading Edge™ fonts
in 9px

Right:
RE Antenna in 8px
enlarged

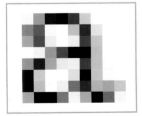

Hyphenation

Currently, automatic hyphenation which is found in DTP programs such as InDesign is still under development. Until this process is completed and we can control justification across all browsers, we have to settle for either ragged text or automatic justification. Justification, however, tends to either contain holes or the browser distributes hyphens across the entire text. For individual critical breaks, a hyphen can be manually inserted between two letters of the text. This resembles the use of soft hyphens in InDesign. The hyphenation of a word or hyphenation at a specific point in the word can be prevented by inserting the character combination ** ** which stands for "non-breaking space." However, this option should be used cautiously as hyphenation will then be deactivated on all devices for all sizes, regardless of whether it is visually required or not.

Blindtext

Nein, meine Texte les ich nicht, so nicht, stöhnte Oxmox. Er war mit Franklin, Rockwell und dem halbtaxgrauen Panther Weidemann in Memphis (Heartbreak Hotel) zugange. Sie warteten auf die fette Gill, um bei der Bank of Helvetica die Kapitälchen in Kapital umzuwandeln. Oxmox liess nicht locker. Ich fleh euch an, rettet meine Copy, gebt meinem Body nochn Durchschuss!

Kein Problem, erbarmte sich Old Face Baskerville, streichelte seinen Hund, zog seine einspaltige Poppl, legte an und traf! (Zeidank nichts Ernstes nurn bisschen Fraktur.) Oxmox: Danke, ist jetzt mit Abstand besser. Derweil jumpte der Fox leise over the Buhl, die sich mal wieder immerdar wie jedes Jahr gesellte. Myriad fragte daraufhin "Biste bescheuert?". Univers rief "um Göttes Willen!". Und Rotis sagte nur "ach, weiß der Teufel". Diesmal war Guaredisch ihr Erwählter, weil seine Laufweite einem vollge-

tankten Bodoni entsprach und seine ungezügelte Unterlänge ihre Serifen so serafisch streifte, dass sie trotz Techtelmechtelei die magere Futura, jene zuverlässige und gern eingesetzte Langstreckenläuferin, rechtsbündig überholen konnten. Leute, giftelte Tiffany, macht endlich main Punkt. Und das Komma soll sich gefällixt an die richtige Stelle setzen. Und keine Trennungen. Und nicht zu viele Anschläge heut nacht! Die Goudy war vorbei. Aus einem üblen Geviert tauchte eine Horde Ge-

3-margin justified text with hyphenations

Ragged text or justification

There is a clear tendency, considering the problem of hyphenation. While justification is generally not recommended, ragged text also has its problems on the Web. A rule of thumb would be to use justification for wide compositions and ragged text for narrow columns. However, these are not fixed rules and should be decided by designers according to the specifications of their projects. Realistically speaking it is only a matter of time until this problem is resolved and we can expect a solution similar to the solution for the serif problem.

In general, headlines on the Web should be indicated by h1, h2, h3, etc. and not designed individually via classes. In this area also, some rules of thumb must be observed.

Tracking/kerning headlines

It is advantageous to kern headlines somewhat. But why? The reasons are obvious – most fonts are optimized for body text. This means that design characteristics for large sizes are embedded in the font. In headlines, readability is not as crucial as for texts in small sizes as enough details are shown for problem-free word recognition. Another key factor is the fact that headlines should not exceed 1–2 lines in most cases.

25px average headline size

A study by Smashing magazine found that most websites operate with headlines that are around 25px. The study recommends using font sizes between 18 and 29px for headlines. It is relatively difficult to find a general rule of thumb for this. Tests of headline sizes of up 70px found that such large headlines can actually be suitable for specific layouts. In recent years in particular there was a general trend towards larger font sizes for body text on the Web, which is why headline sizes should be adjusted accordingly. In the end, this is one of the factors that are left up to the designer to decide and that can be changed according to the application at hand. As a general rule, there should be enough contrast between the head, subhead, and body text to facilitate the orientation of the user on the website. A minor rule that can be derived from this is that particularly large font sizes work best when the individual headlines are short. They should therefore consist of few or short words.

Headline 18px Headline 25px Headline 29px

Double body text height as benchmark for headlines

Another rule of thumb should be treated with caution but offers a good reference point. It says that headlines should be double the size of the body copy. At the same time, the application of the Fibonacci sequence (… 16 – 24 – 40 – 64 – 104 …) or traditional size charts (… 12, 14, 16, 18, 21, 24, 36, 48, 60, 72) are approaches that also lend themselves for use depending on the working method and the design background.

Upper case headlines

As opposed to body copy, the use of upper case is not generally inappropriate for headlines. While uppercase characters should be used sparingly, they can certainly add a certain poignancy to the layout. Similar to large font sizes, the use of upper case headlines is best for short lines as larger text volumes are difficult to read in upper case.

Headline in upper case

Once you have selected one or more fonts, you should be aware that potentially different styles will be needed to emphasize text, etc.

Mixed fonts

In general, similar rules as in print apply. A good reference point is primarily provided by the font classification system according to the form principles by Hans Peter Willberg. In this matrix, the fonts are divided into rows and columns in which the fonts of a single line may not be mixed while mixing fonts within a column can be quite attractive. However, each designer has a personal favorite classification, which is why this topic is rather subjective. Some of the fonts that are standard in print are not used on screen. The small sizes of fonts that belong to static Antiqua according to Willberg or classic Antiqua according to DIN 16518 are rather difficult to read in small sizes. In large sizes, nevertheless these fonts also have some problems, as the luminance of the screen makes the white appear much brighter than in print, and as a result the counters appear larger and the strokes appear thinner. This is considerably more detrimental to the already more difficult to present fonts than to others.

Emphasis and links

Everything is nice and easy in print. There are a multitude of style options available: whether typeface, font, size, color or underscore – there are no limits to the layout. While the same options are available on the Web, much more factors must be considered separately from each other in the hierarchy than with print products. Menu items, hyperlinks, footers, author's information, information such as the date, as well as the classical elements of print layout must be visually separated to allow users to find their way around later. On most websites hyperlinks are identified either by underscoring or color, or even both. Sub-headlines are usually bold and headlines are larger than those commonly used in print. On many websites the actual navigation structure uses a different font size or even a different font. This is why it is more important on the Web than in print to think ahead of all the text categories that will be used in the layout, even if it is only the date of a published article. If these individual categories are written down and sorted prior to the actual layout, fonts can already be allocated to them to create a clearly structured hierarchy later on.

Italics

Another category of font styles that was shunned for a long time on the Web, italics also had the reputation of poor representation on low resolution monitors. Yet the development of various new hinting technologies, especially the PostScript support of display fonts (suitable for headlines) by Typekit, supported the use of italics. These are now better readable even at small sizes. Soon, italics will also be available for use as readily as all other fonts on the Web, with only the standard problems of rasterizers, etc. remaining.

A small tip:
Many vertical italics can be adjusted easier to the quadratic pixel raster and thus displayed better. However, this is only effective if longer text passages are set in italics. In our opinion, for individual words, the slightly diminished presentation quality can be neglected, depending on the font size.

Multiple columns

For a long time, multiple columns were considered to be an absolute no-go on the Web. It is still true that on screen we tend to read downwards rather than from left to right and horizontal arrangements are usually interpreted as different text categories such as information boxes, menus, links, etc. However, technical developments also contributed to enabling multiple columns on the Web today. With JavaScript solutions, for example, columns can be designed in such a way that they automatically add a new column if the minimum width is not reached for a specific display size. These experimental layout variations, however, can only be recommended for experienced designers as they require much more finesse and typographical awareness than standard web layouts.

Hotel) zugange. Sie warteten auf die fette Gill, um bei der Bank of Helvetica die Kapitälchen in Kapital umzuwandeln. Oxmox liess nicht locker.	Diesmal war Guaredisch ihr Erwählter, weil seine Laufweite einem vollgetankten Bodoni entsprach und seine ungezügelte Unterlänge	nacht! Die Goudy war vorbei. Aus einem üblen Geviert tauchte eine Horde Gemeiner auf, angeführt von einem Versalen. Als sie des Grauwerts anblickig

Color is a very subjective design element. As it affects the entire look of a page, it is recommended to deliberately apply color in the initial layout rather than change the color once the whole page has been set up. The color should also underline the hierarchy of the page. It should not counteract it under any circumstances.

Font color

The contrast ratio on screen is different from what we are used to with ink and paper. On the Web there is no need to use the greatest possible contrast; instead the font can be toned down to approximately 80-percent gray, i.e. #333 or #444.

Background color

Once again it is all about the contrast. Inverse compositions, i.e. a white font on black background, are generally less recommended as it limits readability and the fonts are rasterized differently. However, it should not be discarded from the outset. On a website with generally short sentences in which the visual appearance plays a larger role than the readability of long texts, inverse compositions can have an appealing effect. Nevertheless this is also a design element that requires a rather higher degree of finesse and more intense optimization of the font than other layout approaches.

White font with dark grey background and black font with light grey background

Dunkleres Grau 3; #363636

Nein, meine Texte les ich nicht, so nicht, stöhnte Oxmox. Er war mit Franklin, Rockwell und dem halbtaxgrauen Panther Weidemann in Memphis (Heartbreak Hotel) zugange. Sie warteten auf die fette Gill, um bei der Bank of Helvetica die Kapitälchen in Kapital umzuwandeln. Oxmox liess nicht locker. Ich fleh euch an, rettet meine Copy, gebt meinem Body nochn Durchschuss! Kein Problem, erbarmte sich Old Face Baskerville, streichelte seinen Hund, zog seine einspaltige Poppl, legte an und traf! (Zeidank nichts Ernstes nurn bisschen Fraktur.) Oxmox: Danke, ist jetzt mit Abstand besser. Derweil jumpte der Fox leise over the Buhl, die sich mal wieder immerdar wie jedes Jahr gesellte. Diesmal war Guaredisch ihr Erwählter, weil seine Laufweite einem vollgetankten Bodoni entsprach und seine ungezügelte Unterlänge ihre Serifen so serafisch streifte, dass sie trotz Techtelmechtelei die magere Futura, jene zuverlässige und gern eingesetzte Langstreckenläuferin, rechtsbündig überholen konnten. Leute, giftelte Tiffany, macht endlich maln Punkt. Und das Komma soll sich gefällixt an die richtige Stelle setzen. Und keine Trennungen. Und nicht zu viele Anschläge heut nacht! Die Goudy war vorbei. Aus einem üblen Geviert tauchte eine Horde Gemeiner auf,

Helles Grau 3; #EEEEE

Nein, meine Texte les ich nicht, so nicht, stöhnte Oxmox. Er war mit Franklin, Rockwell und dem halbtaxgrauen Panther Weidemann in Memphis (Heartbreak Hotel) zugange. Sie warteten auf die fette Gill, um bei der Bank of Helvetica die Kapitälchen in Kapital umzuwandeln. Oxmox liess nicht locker. Ich fleh euch an, rettet meine Copy, gebt meinem Body nochn Durchschuss! Kein Problem, erbarmte sich Old Face Baskerville, streichelte seinen Hund, zog seine einspaltige Poppl, legte an und traf! (Zeidank nichts Ernstes nurn bisschen Fraktur.) Oxmox: Danke, ist jetzt mit Abstand besser. Derweil jumpte der Fox leise over the Buhl, die sich mal wieder immerdar wie jedes Jahr gesellte. Diesmal war Guaredisch ihr Erwählter, weil seine Laufweite einem vollgetankten Bodoni entsprach und seine ungezügelte Unterlänge ihre Serifen so serafisch streifte, dass sie trotz Techtelmechtelei die magere Futura, jene zuverlässige und gern eingesetzte Langstreckenläuferin, rechtsbündig überholen konnten. Leute, giftelte Tiffany, macht endlich maln Punkt. Und das Komma soll sich gefällixt an die richtige Stelle setzen. Und keine Trennungen. Und nicht zu viele Anschläge heut nacht! Die Goudy war vorbei. Aus einem üblen Geviert tauchte eine Horde Gemeiner auf, angeführt von einem Versalen. Als sie des Grauwerts anblickig wurden, machten sie auf dem Absatz kehrt – ohne Einzug. Die in der letzten Reihe

"Readability doesn't ask simply ›can you read it?‹ It asks, ›do you want to read it‹."

Jason Santa Maria (Creative Director, Typekit)

Text Forms and Reading Patterns on the Web

From the print sector, we have become accustomed to control typography up to the minutest detail. On the Web, however, due to the seemingly endless array of end devices, resolutions and operating systems, we can never be sure when, where and how the user views our contents. This is why it is important to make some preliminary remarks about text forms and reading patterns.

As we cannot manually readjust every alignment and character pair, the macro-typography has to already accommodate the needs of the reader in the design. Depending on the content of the website, it must be adjusted to support the target audience's reading patterns.

In their book "Lesetypografie" (typography of reading), Hans Peter Willberg and Friedrich Forssman introduced reading categories that describe such patterns. We will use these categories as the basis of our discussion and add some screen-specific components. Publishing a text on the Internet today is only a matter of a few clicks. Texts can be published in ways that were not possible on paper. At the same time, there are texts that cannot be adopted one-to-one from the printed form.

Today, written conversations are no longer simple accumulations of questions and answers but usually consist of a range of contributions and remarks. Colors, highlighting, evaluations, pictures, and other design elements help us to keep track of the conversation, even if it extends across several sites, posts, etc. While these text forms seem quite natural to most of us today, they nevertheless follow their own rules and require analysis.

As texts on screen devices follow other rules than their print equivalents, we do not generally adopt the opinion of Willberg and Forssman, but divide the Web into texts and reading patterns that are relevant to us.

In print media, the majority of texts that we read are linear. At least this is what we usually believe. Linear reading denotes reading texts in one go without skipping passages and without searching for specific information. Even if we usually assume that texts are read from A to Z without skipped passages or pauses, this actually only applies to a minority of texts.

The standard example is print fiction, the so-called "reader". As this was the hub of many typographical developments, many of our typographical habits are based on it. Typical of this medium are serif fonts with ragged margins with 60 to 70 characters per line. The aim is to create a smooth reading flow. At the same time, contrasts are usually weak. Compared to other texts, however, line lengths of 70 to 80 characters are also frequently found. To balance this out, they are composed with a slightly increased leading. These rules are rarely applied in web typography for several reasons.

From visiting thousands of websites in the past few years, we have learned that serif fonts are not at home on the Web. However, the fact that the actual technical reason for this – that serif fonts are not rendered very well on screens – has been resolved for many years is often ignored. As this design principal is already firmly established, serif fonts seem inappropriate on the Web. While the line length still applies as a general rule of thumb online, it is nevertheless much harder to control than in print media due to the flexibility of websites (responsive design).

Similar to the line length, the line alignment, the even distribution of line endings with different lengths on the right margin, is hard to control online. Anyone who is familiar with web typography probably came across the rule of "no ragged margins on the Web." There is hope that with improved technology the right margin can actually become controllable. However, as long as not all browsers support hyphenation, ragged margins should actually be used only very cautiously on the Web.

Let us go back to our reading patterns. We now know the typographical characteristics of such a linear readable continuous text and where this type of text is found in the world of print. Yet we know nothing about its counterpart on the Web.

The simple reason: there is none. While there are texts of different lengths that are intended to be read at one go, they usually are read with a basic motivation that is different from reading fiction. Of course, e-books are the one-to-one transition of this reading pattern to screen media, but for us web typography practitioners it is only of marginal importance, as e-books are usually read on specifically conceived devices with their own technical rules. The closest to fiction on the Web are columns from which the readers are

Nein, meine Texte les ich nicht, so nicht, stöhnte Oxmox. Er war mit Franklin, Rockwell und dem halbtaxgrauen Panther Weidemann in Memphis (Heartbreak Hotel) zugange. Sie warteten auf die fette Gill, um bei der Bank of Helvetica die Kapitälchen in Kapital umzuwandeln. Oxmox liess nicht locker. Ich fleh euch an, rettet meine Copy, gebt meinem Body nochn Durchschuss! Kein Problem, erbarmte sich Old Face Baskerville, streichelte seinen Hund, zog seine einspaltige Poppl, legte an und traf! (Zeidank nichts Ernstes nurn bisschen Fraktur.) Oxmox: Danke, ist jetzt mit Abstand besser. Derweil jumpte der Fox leise over the Buhl, die sich mal wieder immerdar wie jedes Jahr geselle. Diesmal war Guaredisch ihr Erwählter, weil seine Laufweite einem vollgetankten Bodoni entsprach und seine ungezügelte Unterlänge ihre Serifen so serafisch streifte, dass sie trotz Techtelmechtelei di magere Futura, jene zuverlässige und gern eingesetzte Langstreckenläuferin, rechtsbündig überholen konnten. Leute, giftelte Tiffany, macht endlich maln Punkt. Und das Komma soll sich gefällixt an die richtige Stelle setzen. Und keine Trennungen. Und nicht zu viele Anschläge heut nacht! Die Goudy war vorbei. Aus einem üblen Geviert tauchte eine Horde Gemeiner auf, angeführt von einem Versalen. Als sie des Grauwerts anblickig wurden, machten sie auf dem Absatz kehrt – ohne Einzug. Die in der letzten Reihe warfen noch schnell eine Handvoll Buchstaben in die Luft, blind darauf vertrauend, dass...

Nein, meine Texte les ich nicht, so nicht, stöhnte Oxmox. Er war mit Franklin, Rockwell und dem halbtaxgrauen Panther Weidemann in Memphis (Heartbreak Hotel) zugange. Sie warteten auf die fette Gill, um bei der Bank of Helvetica die Kapitälchen in Kapital umzuwandeln. Oxmox liess nicht locker. Ich fleh euch an, rettet meine Copy, gebt meinem Body nochn Durchschuss! Kein Problem, erbarmte sich Old Face Baskerville, streichelte seinen Hund, zog seine einspaltige Poppl, legte an und traf! (Zeidank nichts Ernstes nurn bisschen Fraktur.) Oxmox: Danke, ist jetzt mit Abstand besser. Derweil jumpte der Fox leise over the Buhl, die sich mal wieder immerdar wie jedes Jahr geselle. Diesmal war Guaredisch ihr Erwählter, weil seine Laufweite einem vollgetankten Bodoni entsprach und seine ungezügelte Unterlänge ihre Serifen so serafisch streifte, dass sie trotz Techtelmechtelei die magere Futura, jene zuverlässige und gern eingesetzte Langstreckenläuferin, rechtsbündig überholen konnten. Leute, giftelte Tiffany, macht endlich maln Punkt. Und das Komma soll sich gefällixt an die richtige Stelle setzen. Und keine Trennungen. Und nicht zu viele Anschläge heut nacht! Die Goudy war vorbei. Aus einem üblen Geviert tauchte eine Horde Gemeiner auf, angeführt von einem Versalen. Als sie des Grauwerts anblickig wurden, machten sie auf dem Absatz kehrt – ohne Einzug. Die in der letzten Reihe warfen noch schnell eine Handvoll Buchstaben in die

Ragged margin and justified text with a marking at 90 characters per line

not hoping to gain precise information but only read them out of interest in the story.

To decide how a text should be composed it is crucial to know what type of text it is and why it is read.

For example, people may read a travel report because they know the person and want to know how they are doing, or because they are looking for information about a hotel, a vacation site, etc. The first would be categorized under linear reading, while in the second example the reader only skims over the text in search of specific information.

This type of skimming is one of the main reading patterns on the Web. Be it because the readers are in search for the solution to a problem and read a tutorial, because they are skimming news reports in search of exciting articles, or because they are in search for an answer to a question. One reason why we mainly consume text this way is very simple: we do not have time and even if we do, the temptation to be sidetracked is constantly there as everything is only a click away.

We must therefore succeed in catering to this type of reading through typography. We must ensure that readers remain on our page for as long as possible and read a large amount of text before they "bounce" – i.e. move onto another page.

This erratic reading can be divided into different categories that are often found on a single website.

News and summary pages

Many content-oriented websites have a navigation page of sorts that mainly contains teaser texts, preview pictures, etc. and that gives the user a preview of the actual articles. They are usually multi-column with a uniform height and uniform elements (image, text, graphics. etc.)

The obvious print equivalent to this is the classic daily newspaper. Even though we are familiar with teasers and informative images from this medium, they serve a different purpose. On a newspaper page, all articles including all pictures are always fully shown. Even if a headline or image does not appeal to us there, when skimming the page we might come upon an appealing text or a photo caption points out something that we would not have noticed otherwise.

Since on the Web such contents are usually separated by clicks, there are usually only around 50 characters and an image available to draw the user to the actual article. It is therefore important to choose expressive and informative headlines. It is even more important to separate the individual topics from each other. Large spacing to previous and following articles should be observed. Color-coding can also be used. Headlines, links, teasers, photo captions, etc. should be clearly separated from each other to create a clear hierarchy.

A user who does not know right away what the topic is and where to continue reading either scrolls on or moves to another website.

Another important issue is the use of images, which can be used to clearly separate the individual sections.

Another feature that does not exist in the real world is the so-called mouseover or hover effect. This term describes the change of an element if the cursor is moved immediately on top of it. Usually this changes the color, shape, size, or transparency. However, entire elements such as navigation, images, captions, etc. can be shown or removed. For example, on overview pages, initially only images and headlines are shown and only the hover function reveals the introductory text.

Therefore, the most important design factor for news and overview pages is the clear separation of text segments in conjunction with an enlarged headline that would not be required in this size inside an article.

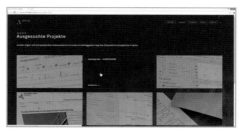

Portfolio of the Achtender agency, in which typography plays a very minor role

Change of an element by a two-step hover (mouseover) effect, www.departmentone.com

Articles about specific topics

As already described for the travel report above, identical content can be read in various ways. It is therefore important to ask two questions up front: **"What does the reader want to learn?"** and **"Why is the reader reading this?"**

The two questions sound very similar, but the motivation is a key factor.

- is the text being read because the reader "has to" read it, possibly as research for the job, university or school,
- is it being read because the topic is currently relevant in the sector and the reader wants to stay up-to-date,
- is it being read because the reader is generally interested in the topic but has not come across the information of the article yet,
- is the reader in search of precise information,
- or is it being read for pure entertainment purposes.

If the majority of the texts of a page fall into the latter category, then it is perfectly all right to use the style elements of fiction and create an even composition with little contrast, long lines, no subheadings, and longer paragraphs.

Whenever this is not the case, things get interesting. If most articles on a page are informative in nature, offering very specific information, it is important to structure them accordingly. This means short paragraphs, clear highlights, and topic-based divisions through many subheadings. Some examples of this include classic tutorials, field reports, etc. They are intended to allow users to reach precisely the information they are looking for through a visual or full-text search (browser search function).

The Internet offers the opportunity of directing users who are still interested in the topic to more elaborate articles or pages with relevant contents. On a standard basis, links, check boxes, lists, images, etc. are used for this purpose. This serves two purposes: on the one hand, users remain on the page after they have received the information they were looking for, while on the other hand, readers who are searching for specific answers are directly addressed and do not move on because they assume the page content is not of interest to them.

However, if the texts are informative and explain contexts in-stead of discussing precise problems, in this type of text there is a higher chance that the reader is reading it out of professional or private interest and wants to understand the topic at hand than with other types of texts.

In such a case, it is important to create a very clear structure for the text. This means: subheads can be a little more elaborate and texts a bit longer. In this case also, background information such as images, statistics and links can be used considerably more frequently in the text as it is assumed that the entire topic is relevant and not just a part of it. At the same time, there is the danger that users come upon information they are already familiar with, which they skip and later lack the exact context, or that they become hooked on linked contents and leave the original page. In former times, when we purchased a specialized book for € 80 and more, the price itself was incentive enough to read it thoroughly and it was also an indication that the reader was interested in the subject.

Today, informative texts are available everywhere on the Internet and if we decide that it is not worthwhile to read the entire text all we have lost is a bit of time and we can quickly and conveniently switch to something more interesting.

This is why it is of particular importance to develop a system for this type of text. This means for example:

- What do my headlines look like?
- What is the relationship among the different headline types such as h1 (most important headline) h2 and h3?
- Does the font size change, as is most commonly used, or can a change in color, font style or the use of small caps make the distinction even better and more intuitive?

Terminology and theme structuring pages

In the print sector, this category would include, for example, encyclopedias. While these are an essential part of the Web in the shape of Wikis, they are not the only relevant type of text. Practically every website has general terms and conditions, entry rules for promotions or FAQs, in which classic question and answer texts are found. In these texts, it is important that the navigation helps users find precisely what they are looking for. For this reason, such sites usually have various types of submenus that allow users to entirely skip all non-relevant contents. In this case, also, highlighting by size, color, and font is more important than inside the article. To support this structuring, web-exclusive technologies, such as the above-mentioned mouseover function or concealing the text and displaying it only one paragraph at a time (accordion effect) can be used.

Picture galleries

Picture galleries can be added to almost any type of online text. Compared to print, they offer advantages and disadvantages. A clear advantage is that only very small preview pictures (thumbnails) can be used without having to plan an entire double-page spread for pictures.The actual text flow is not interrupted much and users can immediately see whether the pictures are relevant to them or not. However, a major disadvantage is what takes place when users actually click on a gallery. This pulls them completely out of the text, directs them to another page, or forces them to close a window that they have opened. There is great danger that users drop out during this process and therefore picture galleries should be used very carefully.

In general, it is usually better to use individual pictures in the text and add a gallery at the end. At the same time, typography of galleries or individual pictures must not be neglected. Especially for pictures whose content is not self-explanatory, it is very important that the caption can be immediately found and is easy to read to offer a quick explanation. While a good picture says more than a thousand words, an abstract picture requires quite a few words to explain.

Commentary pages

Comments fields are a frequently disregarded text category. Even though we have little control over them due to the use of various plug-ins and tools such as Wordpress, Facebook, or forum plug-ins, it is important to at least think about their general appearance.

In the print sector, interviews and letters to the editor are the only equivalent form in which a question and an answer are shown directly underneath each other. The Internet on the other hand, has trained us to follow a conversation between two users even if it is interrupted by other conversation segments. In this case, it is important to focus much more on quotes than in other texts, as it is usually the reference point for continuing the conversation.

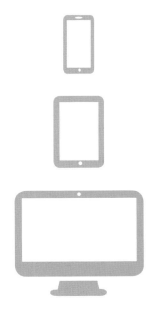

The role of the end device

Even if we believe that the greatest part of the contents that are viewed on a mobile device are identical to the desktop version of the page, it is legitimate and important to shift the focus of the contents on mobile devices. For example, longer texts are read much less frequently on mobile phones than on tablets or PCs. Yet pictures play a much larger role on mobile phones. At the same time, on the mobile phone users usually search for specific information, which is more difficult with the limited space. If the website is supposed to work well even on the smallest mobile devices, it is important to first focus on these devices and then add elements such as sidebars, etc., for larger devices.

This approach is called "mobile first" and unfortunately often disregarded. Yet if a concept works well on a 5 x 10 cm display, it is easy to simply add elements to it for larger screens.

The font should also be changed, which is why it is important to think about the concept ahead of implementation. As the limited space prevents a line length of 45–75 characters with a normal font size, it should be adjusted accordingly.

Yet it would be much more important and effective to resort to condensed fonts for small screens. As these devices are usually operated from a much closer distance than a PC, laptop, or tablet, the character width and character height can be more compact than the desktop variations.

At the end of this chapter we would like to quote our friend, author Jonathan Blum, who exclusively writes online texts, who said

"On the Web, the biggest problem is not to utilize the infinite possibilities that are available".

When it comes to typography, this is best achieved by becoming aware up front of all requirements that should be met by the layout and the font.

Font Analysis

Finding a suitable font for a project is a process including many considerations that will later facilitate everyday work.

If a font is intended for use on the Web or even mobile apps, the designer not only has to carefully select the font but also test its suitability for every desired application. Modern programs such as Typetester or Webfonter offer excellent tools that can be used to test the fonts in a real environment. *(for more information see the chapter Tools for Web Typography, p. 100)*

When the selected font is embedded and displayed in a real environment, the right background information and a trained eye help in quickly analyzing the key features to determine whether it is suited for use in the desired project.

This chapter offers an analysis of diverse fonts with various styles as examples of different font characteristics. A selection ranging from classic print fonts, via popular free fonts up to a font that was specifically designed for use in small sizes on the Web, illustrates the drawbacks and advantages of specific fonts and font styles.

Each font was tested and analyzed regarding its hinting, tracking, glyph shape and x-height, operating system compatibility, as well as its use in large and small sizes.

Rating example
(max. ★★★★★)

Hinting:
★★★★★
Glyph shape:
★★★★★
X-height:
★★★★★
OS consistency:
★★★★★
Small sizes:
★★★★★
Large sizes:
★★★★★
Tracking:
★★★★★

Weights:
Thin, Light, Regular, Semibold, Bold, Extrabold, Heavy

Styles:
Normal & Italic

Adelle	*José Scaglione & Veronika Burian, TypeTogether, 2009, distributed by Typekit*
Antenna	*Cyrus Highsmith, Reading Edge™ Series, Font Bureau, 2007, distributed by Fonts.com*
Bembo®	*Stanley Morison, Monotype, 1929 (original 1495), distributed by Fonts.com*
Calluna	*Jos Buivenga, Exljbris, 2010, distributed by Exljbris*
Depot New Web	*Chris Dickinson, Moretype, 2010, distributed by Typekit*
Gill Sans®	*Eric Gill, Monotype, 1926, distributed by Fonts.com*
Lintel	*Jonathan Hill, The Northern Block, 2006, distributed by The Northern Block and Dafont*
Lobster	*Pablo Impallari, 2010, available license-free from Google Fonts*
Museo Sans	*Jos Buivenga, Exljbris, 2010, distributed by Exljbris*
Open Sans	*Steve Matteson, 2010, available license-free from Google Fonts*
Source Sans Pro	*Paul D. Hunt, 2012, available license-free from Google Fonts or GitHub*
Ubuntu	*Büro Dalton Maag, 2010, available license-free from Ubuntu*

Adelle

In 2009, José Scaglione and Veronika Burian published the modern slab serif typeface Adelle, which was conceived primarily for print magazine use.

Adelle was introduced by their own foundry TypeTogether. As it soon became the most popular web font of TypeTogether, the two designers slightly updated it for better screen rendering.

The character of the slab serif typeface can be described as almost condensed. Its x-height is slightly elevated compared to other typefaces, but in a moderate way. On the Web, in particular this gives it a nice counter opening and an overall friendly character.

Adelle has a total of seven weights from Thin to Heavy, each with a normal and an italic style. However, in the heavier weights the overall layout looks rather tight as the letters from Semibold in OS X and Bold in Windows 7 tend to quickly run into each other. In general, its tracking is a bit lacking and must be increased for on-screen use, as even in 13px regular in Windows the serifs tend to overlap.

The hinting of Adelle is surprisingly good. In enlarged screenshots of 13px, 19px and 40px its shape remains constant and it looks very well balanced in the small sizes in particular. Up to approximately 16px it performs consistently well across all operating systems and only above 16px it suffers from the "OS X disease" of heavier rendering.

However, with slightly increased tracking, which of course needs to be higher for small sizes than for large ones, and primarily in reading sizes, it is well suited for body text. The fact that a font appears heavier on OS X can be neglected if it is used as a headline. This is particularly true if the headline is short, stands alone, and optimal readability is of no particular significance.

José Scaglione & Veronika Burian, TypeTogether, 2009, distributed by Typekit

Rating
(max. ★★★★★)

Hinting:
★★★★★

Glyph shape:
★★★★★

X-height:
★★★

OS consistency:
★★★★

Small sizes:
★★★★★

Large sizes:
★★★

Tracking:
★

Weights:
Thin, Light, Regular, Semibold, Bold, Extrabold, Heavy

Styles:
Normal & Italic

*Enlarged depiction of the lowercase "a" of Adelle,
based on 8px, 19px and vector (from left to right)*

Anyone searching for a font to combine with Adelle with a similar character can go the easy way and select Adelle Sans which was created to match Adelle. According to the creators, in Adelle Sans all styles are manually hinted to ensure better screen rendering.

Adelle Thin 100	The five boxing wizard
Adelle Thin Italic 100	*Brawny gods just flock*
Adelle Light 300	Waltz, bad nymph, for
Adelle Light Italic 300	*Vamp fox held quartz*
Adelle Regular 400	The five boxing wizard
Adelle Italic 400	*Brawny gods just flock*
Adelle Semibold 600	Waltz, bad nymph, for
Adelle Semibold Italic 600	*Vamp fox held quartz*
Adelle Bold 700	**The five boxing wizar**
Adelle Bold Italic 700	***Brawny gods just floc***
Adelle Extrabold 800	**Waltz, bad nymph, for**
Adelle Extrabold Italic 800	***Vamp fox held quartz***
Adelle Heavy 900	**The five boxing wizar**
Adelle Heavy Italic 900	***Brawny gods just floc***

Nein, meine Texte les ich nicht, so nicht, stöhnte Oxmox. Er war mit Franklin, Rockwell und dem halbtaxgrauen Panther Weidemann in Memphis (Heartbreak Hotel) zugange. Sie warteten auf die fette Gill, um bei der Bank of Helvetica die Kapitälchen in Kapital umzuwandeln. Oxmox liess nicht locker. Ich fleh euch an, rettet meine Copy, gebt meinem Body nochn Durchschuss! Kein Problem, erbarmte sich Old Face Baskerville, streichelte seinen Hund, zog seine einspaltige Poppl, legte an und traf! (Zeidank nichts Ernstes nurn bisschen Fraktur.) Oxmox: Danke, ist jetzt mit Abstand besser. Derweil jumpte der Fox leise over den Buhl, die sich mal wieder immerdar wie jedes Jahr gesellte. Diesmal war Guaredisch ihr Erwählter, weil seine Laufweite einem vollgetankten Bodoni entsprach und

Screenshot (OS X) of a body text as it is depicted on the Web

Antenna

Antenna was designed by the US font foundry The Font Bureau, whose Reading Edge™ Series was created to precisely address the problems analyzed here – font rendering on screens.

While the series catalog contains only eight typefaces so far, their hinting is almost unparalleled by other offers. They are especially optimized for sizes from 9px to 18px and hinted separately at every pixel level.

Antenna itself has an almost square shape. It is also distinguished by its high x-height and very short descenders. Similar to Lintel it has oval counters. However, they are not as extremely prominent and come to play mostly in the light styles. Even in the smaller sizes of problem letters such as "e" and "a", there is enough room for shape development.

The italics are only calculated and there are no alternative glyphs (such as the single-story "a"). However, since Antenna was primarily conceived as an extremely robust body font and italics are mainly used for mark-ups, this does not negatively affect practical application much.

At the same time, the bold and bold italic styles suffer from the same problems of tapering counters, especially the lowercase "a" and "e". Yet since it is practically natural for the counters to decrease if the weight increases, this may be annoying but realistically speaking practically unavoidable.

The stroke of Antenna is always constant within a single weight, which further enhances its good line characteristics and robust nature. While it is rather unlikely that it will actually be used in 8px, for websites that require the rendering of large amounts of text, it is the ideal body font. If one takes into account the effort required to develop a typeface with such qualities, then the price, which is slightly above others, is certainly justified.

Cyrus Highsmith, Reading Edge™ Series, Font Bureau, 2007, distributed by Fonts.com

Rating
(max. ★★★★★)

Hinting:
★★★★★
Glyph shape:
★★★
X-height:
★★★★★
OS consistency:
★★★★★
Small sizes:
★★★★★
Large sizes:
★★★★★
Tracking:
★★★★★

Weights:
Regular, Bold

Styles:
Normal & Italic

Also available at MyFonts, FontShop and Typekit

Enlarged depiction of the lowercase "a" of Antenna, based on 8px, 19px and vector (from left to right)

According to the distributing website, the Reading Edge™ fonts with their designs and special characteristics are directly related to the core web fonts Georgia and Verdana.

Antenna RE   Pack my box with five dozen liqu

Antenna RE Italic   *Pack my box with five dozen liqu*

Antenna RE Bold   **Pack my box with five dozen liqu**

Antenna RE Bold Italic   ***Pack my box with five dozen liqu***

Nein, meine Texte les ich nicht, so nicht, stöhnte Oxmox. Er war mit Franklin, Rockwell und dem halbtaxgrauen Panther Weidemann in Memphis (Heartbreak Hotel) zugange. Sie warteten auf die fette Gill, um bei der Bank of Helvetica die Kapitälchen in Kapital umzuwandeln. Oxmox liess nicht locker. Ich fleh euch an, rettet meine Copy, gebt meinem Body nochn Durchschuss! Kein Problem, erbarmte sich Old Face Baskerville, streichelte seinen Hund, zog seine einspaltige Poppl, legte an und traf! (Zeidank nichts Ernstes nurn bisschen Fraktur.) Oxmox: Danke, ist jetzt mit Abstand besser. Derweil jumpte der Fox leise over den Buhl, die sich mal wieder immerdar wie jedes Jahr gesellte. Diesmal war Guaredisch ihr Erwählter, weil seine Laufweite einem vollgetankten Bodoni entsprach und seine ungezügelte Unterlänge ihre Serifen so serafisch streifte, dass sie trotz Techtelmechtelei die magere Futura, jene zuverlässige und gern eingesetzte Langstreckenläuferin, rechtsbündig überholen konnten. Leute, giftelte Tiffany, macht endlich maln Punkt. Und das Komma soll sich gefällixt an die richtige Stelle setzen. Und keine Trennungen. Und nicht zu viele Anschläge heut nacht! Die Goudy war vorbei. Aus einem üblen Geviert tauchte eine Horde Gemeiner auf, angeführt von einem Versalen. Als sie des Grauwerts anblickig wurden, machten sie auf dem Absatz kehrt – ohne Einzug. Die in der letzten Reihe warfen noch schnell eine Handvoll Buchstaben in die Luft.

Screenshot (OS X) of a body text as it is depicted on the Web

Bembo®

Examining the on-screen suitability of classical fonts from the print era also provides clues of what to look for.

As one of the first old style serif (Antiqua) typefaces, Bembo® by Francesco Griffo is an excellent example to use. Griffo and Nicolas Jensun, who both worked for Aldus Manutius, are considered the creators of what today is described as the Antiqua (serif) style. Griffo also invented the first cursive typefaces (1502), and this style was subsequently called italics in reference to his nationality. Even though these events took place during the Renaissance in Venice, Bembo® is ironically today referred to as French Renaissance Antiqua since, as opposed to the Venetian Renaissance Antiqua, it has a straight instead of a slanted crossbar. The Bembo® used today was redesigned a few centuries later in 1929 by Stanley Morison for the Monotype Corporation based on Griffo's design.

But let us turn to its use on the Web. Bembo® is distributed by Monotype via its internal hosting service, Fonts.com. As can be expected by a font based on the designs of Griffo, the cursive shapes are really cursive and almost all glyphs contain beautiful alternative styles. However, when testing the font on the Web, a small fault is found in the kerning – under Firefox across all systems letter combinations such as "St" or "Un" are displayed erroneously and with extensive overlap. Apart from that, the stroke variation is relatively limited, which is very suitable to rendering on current screens.

Unfortunately, another key element, the x-height, is relatively low. In very small grades (12px and less), the gray value becomes slightly uneven but remains relatively readable. While the gray value is uniform under OS X, some shapes are nearly lost. This can be observed, for example, in the lowercase "e" in which the crossbar is totally eliminated from 12px and smaller. At the same time, as usual, the font is bolder under OS X, but not overly so. The alternative characters also cause some problems, for example the majuscule "R" used in the

Stanley Morison, Monotype, 1929 (original 1495), distributed by Fonts.com

Rating
(max. ★★★★★)

Hinting:
★★★
Glyph shape:
★★★
X-height:
★★
OS consistency:
★★★
Small sizes:
★★
Large sizes:
★★★★★
Tracking:
★★★★

Weights:
Roman, Semibold, Bold, ExtraBold, Titling

Styles:
Normal & Italic

Enlarged depiction of the lowercase "a" of Bembo®,
based on 8px, 19px and vector (from left to right)

standard character set has a very decorative tail that can quickly cause problems in body copy. In addition, depending on the used monitor, operating system and browser, the font either begins to flicker or loses part of its distinctive shape.

In conclusion, it can be said that Bembo® only causes problems in very small sizes and even with those problems it remains easily readable. Whether it is enjoyable to read is another issue. Applied in larger sizes, especially in the titling versal style developed for this purpose, the distinguishing shape of the characters is fully recovered, which restores Bembo's® historic charm.

Bembo® Roman	The quick brown fox jum
Bembo® Italic	*The quick brown fox jum*
Bembo® Semibold	**The quick brown fox jum**
Bembo® Semibold Italic	***The quick brown fox jum***
Bembo® Bold	**The quick brown fox jum**
Bembo® Bold Italic	***The quick brown fox jum***
Bembo® ExtraBold	**The quick brown fox jum**
Bembo® ExtraBold Italic	***The quick brown fox jum***
Bembo® Titling	THE QUICK BROWN FO:
Bembo® Titling Italic	*THE QUICK BROWN FO*

Nein, meine Texte les ich nicht, so nicht, stöhnte Oxmox. Er war mit Franklin, Rockwell und dem halbtaxgrauen Panther Weidemann in Memphis (Heartbreak Hotel) zugange. Sie warteten auf die fette Gill, um bei der Bank of Helvetica die Kapitälchen in Kapital umzuwandeln. Oxmox liess nicht locker. Ich fleh euch an, rettet meine Copy, gebt meinem Body nochn Durchschuss! Kein Problem, erbarmte sich Old Face Baskerville, streichelte seinen Hund, zog seine einspaltige Poppl, legte an und traf! (Zeidank nichts Ernstes nurn bisschen Fraktur.) Oxmox: Danke, ist jetzt mit Abstand besser. Derweil jumpte der Fox leise over the Buhl, die sich mal wieder immerdar wie jedes Jahr gesellte. Diesmal war Guaredisch ihr Erwählter, weil seine Laufweite einem vollgetankten Bodoni entsprach und seine ungezügelte Unterlänge ihre Serifen so serafisch streifte, dass sie trotz Techtelmechtelei die magere Futura, jene zuverlässige und gern eingesetzte Langstreckenläuferin, rechtsbündig überholen konnten. Leute, giftelte Tiffany, macht endlich maln Punkt. Und das Komma soll sich gefällixt an die richtige Stelle setzen. Und keine Trennungen. Und nicht zu viele Anschläge heut nacht! Die Goudy war vorbei. Aus einem üblen Geviert tauchte eine Horde Gemeiner auf, angeführt von einem Versalen. Als sie des Grauwerts anblickig wurden, machten sie auf dem Absatz kehrt – ohne Einzug. Die in der letzten Reihe warfen noch schnell eine Handvoll

Screenshot (OS X) of a body text as it is depicted on the Web

Calluna

In the cursive styles of his Museo Sans, Jos Bui-venga, the Dutch font artist of Arnheim had neglected some details.

In contrast, in his Calluna typeface he has obviously attend-ed to them. Yet the comparison with Museo is not that far fetched even if the similarities only become apparent upon a second look. Buivenga once said that Calluna was created at a time when he was taking a break from working on Mu-seo. At the time, he started to develop a slab serif form of the Museo shapes (the original Museo and not the Museo Sans also shown here) by adding beaks to the end stems. This resulted in the unmistakable shape details of the serifs that are rounded on one side. To the left, the font has kept the serif brackets of Museo. On the other side, the right-angled beaks that are typical of Egyptienne typefaces are added as serifs. This gives it great dynamism and excellent line readability as the movement seems to continue in the reading direction.

Despite this characteristic, Calluna's shape principles are based on the fonts of the Venetian Renaissance Antiqua, featuring its typical slanted "e". Overall, it rather closely resembles Bembo®, which is why these two typefaces can be easily compared to each other. As opposed to Bembo®, and Renaissance Antiqua fonts in general, Calluna has a very high x-height. The stroke variations, on the other hand, are very classic. On the screen, Calluna creates a very uniform gray value and, as opposed to Bembo®, it does not create holes in the composition. One of the main reasons for this is the standard good hinting of the typefaces of Jos Buivenga. There is a simple trick for examining the hinting of a font. You create a screenshot of a small and an extremely large size of the font, put them next to each other, and scale them to a large scale. If the glyph shapes have the same charac-teristics in the small sizes as in the large depiction without creating a pulp of colored pixels, then more time has been invested in good hinting.

Jos Buivenga, Exljbris, 2010, distributed by Exljbris

Rating
(max. ★★★★★)

Hinting:
★★★★★
Glyph shape:
★★★★★
X-height:
★★★
OS consistency:
★★★★★
Small sizes:
★★★
Large sizes:
★★★★★
Tracking:
★★★

Weights:
Light, Regular, Semi-bold, Bold, Black

Styles:
*Normal & Italic
(Light and Black only available in normal)*

Also available at My-Fonts, FontShop and Typekit

Enlarged depiction of the lowercase "a" of Calluna, based on 8px, 19px and vector (from left to right)

There is another reason for a uniform gray value in the composition – the actual shape of the letters. The open counters, i.e. the bottom "e" bow , the top "a" bow, the "u" counter, or the serifs facing each other in the "w", are all kept very light. This allows the font to develop its character even in small sizes. A positive outcome of this is that, as opposed to other fonts, in small sizes the top "w" serifs do not blend into a single bar. Nevertheless, in Calluna the natural tracking is also not enough for screen rendering, especially in small sizes.

Overall, Calluna is a beautiful font. It is proof that there are modern serif fonts that are not true slab serif fonts.

Calluna Light 300

Calluna Normal 400

Calluna Italic 400

Calluna Semibold 600

Calluna Semibold Italic 600

Calluna Bold 700

Calluna Bold Italic 700

Calluna Black 900

The five boxing wiza

Brawny gods just floc

Waltz, bad nymph, fo

Vamp fox held quart

The five boxing wizar

Brawny gods just flo

Waltz, bad nymph, fo

Vamp fox held quar

Nein, meine Texte les ich nicht, so nicht, stöhnte Oxmox. Er war mit Franklin, Rockwell und dem halbtaxgrauen Panther Weidemann in Memphis (Heartbreak Hotel) zugange. Sie warteten auf die fette Gill, um bei der Bank of Helvetica die Kapitälchen in Kapital umzuwandeln. Oxmox liess nicht locker. Ich fleh euch an, rettet meine Copy, gebt meinem Body nochn Durchschuss! Kein Problem, erbarmte sich Old Face Baskerville, streichelte seinen Hund, zog seine einspaltige Poppl, legte an und traf! (Zeidank nichts Ernstes nurn bisschen Fraktur.) Oxmox: Danke, ist jetzt mit Abstand besser. Derweil jumpte der Fox leise over the Buhl, die sich mal wieder immerdar wie jedes Jahr gesellte. Diesmal war Guaredisch ihr Erwählter, weil seine Laufweite einem vollgetankten Bodoni entsprach und seine ungezügelte Unterlänge ihre Serifen so serafisch streifte, dass sie trotz Techtelmechtelei die magere Futura, jene zuverlässige und gern eingesetzte Langstreckenläuferin, rechtsbündig überholen konnten. Leute, giftelte Tiffany, macht endlich maln Punkt. Und das Komma soll sich gefällixt an die richtige Stelle setzen. Und keine Trennungen. Und nicht zu viele Anschläge heut nacht! Die Goudy war vorbei. Aus einem üblen Geviert tauchte eine Horde Gemeiner auf, angeführt von einem Versalen. Als sie des Grauwerts anblickt wurden, machten sie

Screenshot (OS X) of a body text as it is depicted on the Web

Depot New Web

Depot New Web is a font family distributed by Typekit that was designed by Chris Dickinson and introduced by his foundry Moretype.

Chris Dickinson, Moretype, 2010, distributed by Typekit

Rating
(max. ★★★★★)

Hinting:
★★
Glyph shape:
★★★★★
X-height:
★★★★
OS consistency:
★
Small sizes:
★★★
Large sizes:
★★★★★
Tracking:
★★★

Weights:
Thin, Light, Regular, Medium, Bold

Styles:
Normal & Italic

The individual fonts of the font family are excellently suited for on-screen rendering as they are generally very open. For example, the "e" has a wide open counter and the other glyphs also feature similarly large openings. Compared to classic print typefaces such as Helvetica (Max Miefiger), the "f" is only slightly slanted and thus avoids touching the next letter. The font's very open design is particularly obvious in the lowercase "a" and "s".

The x-height is generally slightly elevated, which is only apparent upon closer inspection and is the main reason why the counter could be designed this open. It is thus not a mere style element as, for example, in Vectora (Adrian Frutiger). The rather moderate stroke variation is also an advantage for on-screen rendering.

However, Depot also has some disadvantages that may prohibit its usage in certain layouts or situations. First, similar to most fonts, it features auto-hinting, which causes problems with small font sizes as the consistent rendering of the glyph shapes and counters is not guaranteed in all sizes. At the same time, its natural tracking is somewhat reduced, which, despite the open glyph shapes and descenders, results in the overlapping of glyphs of some kerning pairs.

Compared to the print variation of the font, the tracking on the Web appears slightly reduced, even though the opposite would be preferable. When it comes to rendering across operating systems, the use of Depot requires a special touch. The peculiarity of rendering under OS X comes to play in an extreme way here so that a light weight under OS X appears like a regular weight on Windows. In conclusion, it can be said that Depot is a successful font for web use despite individual technical drawbacks, which in a large font range as the one offered by Typekit are expected to occur in some

Enlarged depiction of the lowercase "a" of Depot New Web, based on 8px, 19px and vector (from left to right)

fonts. When used in slightly larger sizes (approx. 20px), which can be considered a current web design trend, it is a well readable font suitable for everyday use on the Web.

Depot New Web Thin

Depot New Web Thin Italic

Depot New Web Light

Depot New Web Light Italic

Depot New Web Regular

Depot New Web Italic

Depot New Web Medium

Depot New Web Medium Italic

Depot New Web Bold

Depot New Web Bold Italic

Why pangolins dream (

Why pangolins dream (

Why Pangolins dream

Why pangolins dream

Why pangolins dream

Why pangolins dream

Why pangolins dream

Why pangolins dream

Why pangolins dream

Why pangolins dream

halbtaxgrauen Panther Weidemann in Memphis (Heartbreak Hotel) zugange. Sie warteten auf die fette Gill, um bei der Bank of Helvetica die Kapitälchen in Kapital umzuwandeln. Oxmox liess nicht locker. Ich fleh euch an, rettet meine Copy, gebt meinem Body nochn Durchschuss! Kein Problem, erbarmte sich Old Face Baskerville, streichelte seinen Hund, zog seine einspaltige Poppl, legte an und traf! (Zeidank nichts Ernstes nurn bisschen Fraktur.) Oxmox: Danke, ist jetzt mit Abstand besser. Derweil jumpte der Fox leise over the Buhl, die sich mal wieder immerdar wie jedes Jahr gesellte. Diesmal war Guaredisch ihr Erwählter, weil seine Laufweite einem vollgetankten Bodoni entsprach und seine ungezügelte Unterlänge ihre Serifen so serafisch streifte, dass sie trotz Techtelmechtelei die magere Futura, jene zuverlässige und gern eingesetzte Langstreckenläuferin, rechtsbündig überholen konnten. Leute, giftelte Tiffany, macht endlich maln Punkt. Und das Komma soll sich gefällixt an die richtige Stelle setzen. Und keine Trennungen. Und nicht zu viele Anschläge heut nacht! Die Goudy war vorbei. Aus einem üblen Geviert tauchte eine Horde Gemeiner auf, angeführt von einem Versalen. Als sie des Grauwerts anblickig wurden, machten sie auf dem Absatz kehrt – ohne Einzug. Die in der letzten Reihe warfen noch schnell eine Handvoll Buchstaben in die Luft, blind darauf vertrauend, dass...

Screenshot (OS X) of a body text as it is depicted on the Web

Gill Sans®

The good old Gill Sans® has been widely debated. For some experts it is the British Helvetica.

Eric Gill, Monotype, 1926, distributed by Fonts.com

Others primarily look at it as a font that has to be generously tracked to even begin using it.

As the name says, Gill Sans® is based on the designs of the British calligrapher and typographer Eric Gill. In his youth, Gill was a student of the famous British typographer Edward Johnston whom he assisted in designing the typeface for the signs of the London Underground Railway. When Stanley Morison, who was a typographic consultant for Monotype in the early days of the font empire, was in search for new fonts and came across the designs of Gill, he quickly noticed the similarity of the character shapes to the almost iconic font of the London Underground Railway. As he expected such a font to generate very large demand, he worked over the designs together with Gill, while keeping the similarity to the underground railway font, which designers criticize frequently today. Similar to the later developed Helvetica or Univers, Gill Sans® is based on a lightweight humanist shape principle, which was new for sans-serif fonts at the time.

The Gill Sans® described here is distributed by Fonts.com (Monotype) and is available as a free font for websites, at least in some of its variations.

Gill Sans® maintains all its attributes on the Web. However, on the Web of all places, tracking is of key importance and Gill Sans® does not come across favorably: its beautiful open shapes that would make it predestined for on-screen use are destroyed. As opposed to print usage, its light weight is actually expedient on the Web. In medium it is relatively easy to read in small font sizes. The other weights cannot be recommended for use on the Web. The font's characteristic shapes with the great stroke variations, for example in the lowercase "a", quickly become annoying on screen. In

Rating
(max. ★★★★★)

Hinting:
★★
Glyph shape:
★
X-height:
★★★★
OS consistency:
★★★
Small sizes:
★★★★
Large sizes:
★
Tracking:
-

Weights:
Light, Book, Roman, Bold, Heavy

Styles:
Normal & Italic

Enlarged depiction of the lowercase "a" of Gill Sans®, based on 8px, 19px and vector (from left to right)

this becomes so extreme that the combination of narrow tracking and great stroke variations is very irritating. In some uses, especially uppercase letters at the beginning of words, these appear almost blotched in the gray scale. While this is bearable under OS X, under Windows 7, the effect of the low resolution of older monitors becomes even more extreme. Even if the tracking is expanded via CSS, it is very difficult to find the correct settings as it will always look too wide in one place and too narrow in another.

Even if this will probably upset many print graphic designers it must be said that the times of Gill Sans®, at least online and with the current technologies, is over.

Gill Sans® Light — When zombies arrive, quickly

Gill Sans® Light Italic — *When zombies arrive, quickly t*

Gill Sans® Book — When zombies arrive, quickl

Gill Sans® Book Italic — *When zombies arrive, quickly*

Gill Sans® Roman — **When zombies arrive, quick**

Gill Sans® Italic — *When zombies arrive, quickly*

Gill Sans® Bold — **When zombies arrive, quickl**

Gill Sans® Bold Italic — ***When zombies arrive, quickly***

Gill Sans® Heavy — **When zombies arrive, quickly**

Gill Sans® Heavy Italic — ***When zombies arrive, quickly***

Nein, meine Texte les ich nicht, so nicht, stöhnte Oxmox. Er war mit Franklin, Rockwell und dem halbtaxgrauen Panther Weidemann in Memphis (Heartbreak Hotel) zugange. Sie warteten auf die fette Gill, um bei der Bank of Helvetica die Kapitälchen in Kapital umzuwandeln. Oxmox liess nicht locker. Ich fleh euch an, rettet meine Copy, gebt meinem Body nochn Durchschuss! Kein Problem, erbarmte sich Old Face Baskerville, streichelte seinen Hund, zog seine einspaltige Poppl, legte an und traf! (Zeidank nichts Ernstes nurn bisschen Fraktur.) Oxmox: Danke, ist jetzt mit Abstand besser. Derweil jumpte der Fox leise over the Buhl, die sich mal wieder immerdar wie jedes Jahr gesellte. Diesmal war Guaredisch ihr Erwählter, weil seine Laufweite einem vollgetankten Bodoni entsprach und seine ungezügelte Unterlänge ihre Serifen so serafisch streifte, dass sie trotz Techtelmechtelei die magere Futura, jene zuverlässige und gern eingesetzte Langstreckenläuferin, rechtsbündig überholen konnten. Leute, giftelte Tiffany, macht endlich mаln Punkt. Und das Komma soll sich gefällixt an die richtige Stelle setzen. Und keine Trennungen. Und nicht zu viele Anschläge heut nacht! Die Goudy war vorbei. Aus einem üblen Geviert tauchte eine Horde Gemeiner auf, angeführt von einem Versalen. Als sie des Grauwerts anblickig wurden, machten sie auf dem Absatz kehrt – ohne Einzug. Die in der letzten Reihe

Screenshot (OS X) of a body text as it is depicted on the Web

Lintel

Lintel is one of the sans-serif fonts that cannot deny the spirit of the time of its creation. As opposed to the other fonts of the late 1990s however, which Friedrich Forssman described as "Techno fonts," it has a less deformed appearance.

While it has geometric elements, it is far from being a constructed font. Lintel has a very large x-height, as is desirable for screen rendering. However, compared to other fonts this is not achieved by generally creating larger minuscules. Instead, the x-height is simply lifted while keeping the tracking constant. This approach results in very oval-shaped counters, for example for the "o". These open counters considerably contribute to the font's good screen rendering. This open counter style even almost causes the top part of the eye to collide with the top bow in the lowercase "a".

Tracking is similar to most Exljbris fonts, perhaps even a bit more extreme. While Lintel is very suitable to web use, a little more tracking would considerably improve the readability of its small sizes on screen.

However, once all browsers master subpixel tracking enhancement, this point will become less of an issue as manual spacing of a font will become much easier. On the other hand, there is nothing wrong with the hinting of Lintel. During the tests, it was only found that on some computers there are occasional hinting errors. In such cases, in particular for very heavy and very light fonts, individual letters appear much too large or too small compared to the other letters.

At the same time, some bows may be affected by such hinting errors, causing the lowercase "o" to develop a shoulder that looks much heavier than its other parts. This error frequently also occurs in the lowercase "u" under OS X 10.6.7 in Chrome. On other operating systems or browsers, no other hinting errors were found.

Jonathan Hill,
The Northern Block, 2006,
distributed by The Northern Block and Dafont

Rating
(max. ★★★★★)

Hinting:
★★★★★
Glyph shape:
★★★
X-height:
★★★
OS consistency:
★★★★★
Small sizes:
★★★★
Large sizes:
★★★★
Tracking:
★★

Weights:
Light, Regular,
Medium, Bold,
Extra Bold

Styles:
Normal & Italic

Enlarged depiction of the lowercase "a" of Lintel,
based on 8px, 19px and vector (from left to right)

Despite this, it is rather questionable whether Lintel will be used for many practical applications. The very distinguished shapes of this font may be a deterrent from using it for specific projects.

Lintel Light	The quick brown fox jur
Lintel Light Italic	*The quick brown fox ju*
Lintel Regular	The quick brown fox j
Lintel Italic	*The quick brown fox j*
Lintel Medium	The quick brown fox ju
Lintel Medium Italic	*The quick brown fox ju*
Lintel Bold	The quick brown fox ju
Lintel Bold Italic	*The quick brown fox ju*
Lintel Extra Bold	The quick brown fox j
Lintel Extra Bold Italic	*The quick brown fox ju*

Nein, meine Texte les ich nicht, so nicht, stöhnte Oxmox. Er war mit Franklin, Rockwell und dem halbtaxgrauen Panther Weidemann in Memphis (Heartbreak Hotel) zugange. Sie warteten auf die fette Gill, um bei der Bank of Helvetica die Kapitälchen in Kapital umzuwandeln. Oxmox liess nicht locker. Ich fleh euch an, rettet meine Copy, gebt meinem Body nochn Durchschuss! Kein Problem, erbarmte sich Old Face Baskerville, streichelte seinen Hund, zog seine einspaltige Poppl, legte an und trafl (Zeidank nichts Ernstes nurn bisschen Fraktur.) Oxmox: Danke, ist jetzt mit Abstand besser. Derweil jumpte der Fox leise over the Buhl, die sich mal wieder immerdar wie jedes Jahr gesellte. Diesmal war Guaredisch ihr Erwählter, weil seine Laufweite einem vollgetankten Bodoni entsprach und seine ungezügelte Unterlänge ihre Serifen so serafisch streifte, dass sie trotz Techtelmechtelei die magere Futura, jene zuverlässige und gern eingesetzte Langstreckenläuferin, rechtsbündig überholen konnten. Leute, giftelte Tiffany, macht endlich maln Punkt. Und das Komma soll sich gefällixt an die richtige Stelle setzen. Und keine Trennungen. Und nicht zu viele Anschläge heut nachtl Die Goudy war vorbei. Aus einem üblen Geviert tauchte eine Horde Gemeiner auf, angeführt von einem Versalen. Als sie des Grauwerts anblickig wurden, machten sie auf dem

Screenshot (OS X) of a body text as it is depicted on the Web

Lobster

When we talk about fonts we usually talk about copy text and copy text typography. Yet finding a good display font can require as much time and patience.

On the Web in particular, where users often leave pages after briefly scrolling them, headlines are among the most important typographical tools. Lobster, a font developed by the Argentinean font designer Pablo Impallari, is perfectly suited for such display elements including headlines, illustrations of scripts, and, to a certain degree, also photo captions.

It is a very bold cursive script font. Script typefaces resemble handwriting and are often distinguished by connections between the letters and a large range of alternative letters. Currently, they are still not available for all browsers, but are increasingly becoming so.

Lobster has a very high x-height, giving it a powerful distinct look even in small sizes. Its vertical, almost straight stems coupled with very round connections create the distinguished character of this typeface. The eye-catching decorative beaks are an additional distinguishing element that is not found to the same degree in other fonts.

These details with the overly bold stems would definitely be too much for long-form reading texts, but Lobster was not intended for this. It is at its best when placed in a large size with plenty of space at the head of a page where all its hidden details can be fully displayed. Its distinguished character is also the reason for its only two drawbacks. As it is available free of charge on Google Fonts, including all its alternative characters, it is becoming increasingly popular and is therefore used quite frequently. But if it is seen too often, users may become bored with it.

Another drawback is its hinting. Due to the very bold stems and the focus on very large sizes, hinting is almost non-ex-

Pablo Impallari, 2010, available license-free from Google Fonts

Rating
(max. ★★★★★)

Hinting:
★

Glyph shape:
★★★★★

X-height:
★★★★

OS consistency:
★★★★

Small sizes:
★

Large sizes:
★★★★★

Tracking:
★★★★

Weights:
Bold

Styles:
Italic

Also available at Typekit

Enlarged depiction of the lowercase "a" of Lobster, based on 8px, 19px and vector (from left to right)

istent for small sizes. Other than that, Lobster fulfills everything expected from a script font for headlines.

The fact that it is only available in a single style is not really a drawback as headlines rarely require more than a single style. For all those who would like to use more of Lobster, there is also Lobster Two with two upright variants and a lighter weight, which is also found on Google Fonts.

Lobster as Headline font

Lobster as Headline font

Lobster as Headline font

Lobster as Headline font

Lobster as Headline font

Lobster as Headline font

Lobster as Headline font

Lobster as Headline font

Nein, meine Texte les ich nicht, so nicht, stöhnte Oxmox. Er war mit Franklin, Rockwell und dem halbtaxgrauen Panther Weidemann in Memphis (Heartbreak Hotel) zugange. Sie warteten auf die fette Gill, um bei der Bank of Helvetica die Kapitälchen in Kapital umzuwandeln. Oxmox ließ nicht locker. Ich fleh euch an, rettet meine Copy, gebt meinem Body nochn Durchschuss! Kein Problem, erbarmte sich Old Face Baskerville, streichelte seinen Hund, zog seine einspaltige Poppl, legte an und traf! (Zeidank nichts Ernstes - nurn bisschen Fraktur.) Oxmox: Danke, ist jetzt mit Abstand besser. Derweil jumpte der Fox leise over den Buhl, die sich mal wieder immerdar wie jedes Jahr gesellte. Diesmal war Guaredisch ihr Erwählter, weil seine Laufweite einem vollgetankten Bodoni entsprach und seine ungezügelte Unterlänge ihre Serifen so serafisch streifte, dass sie trotz Techtelmechtelei die magere Futura, jene zuverlässige und gern eingesetzte Langstreckenläuferin, rechtsbündig überholen konnten. Leute, giftete Tiffany, macht endlich main Punkt. Und das Komma soll sich gefällist an die richtige Stelle setzen. Und keine Trennungen. Und nicht zu viele Anschläge heut nacht! Die Goudy war vorbei. Aus einem üblen Geviert tauchte eine Horde Gemeiner auf, angeführt von einem Versalen. Als sie des Grauwerts anblickig wurden, machten sie auf dem Absatz kehrt - ohne Einzug. Die in der letzten Reihe warfen noch schnell eine Handvoll Buchstaben in die Luft, blind darauf vertrauend, dass...

Screenshot (OS X) of a body text as it is depicted on the Web

Museo Sans

Some typefaces are unmistakable – Rotis has its lowercase "e" with which it is always identified, Gill Sans® its lowercase "a" and Helvetica its capital "R".

In Museo, it is the minuscules "a" and "k". The character shape of Museo is clearly based on the humanist shape principle, which can be seen very clearly in the uppercase "M", "W", "J", "F", and "E".

Museo was designed by Jos Buivenga and is distributed by his foundry Exljbris. Exljbris became well known for the fact that it offers the fonts of Jos Buivenga either as entire free fonts or at least some font styles free of charge. As opposed to most other free fonts however, these are in excellent quality! The web fonts are available for self-hosting via Fontspring or as an embedded link via Typekit.

While Museo resembles Avenir by Frutiger, as opposed to many other free fonts it is not plagiarized but simply Buivenga's approach to a sans-serif variation with the look of a constructed gothic font. At the same time, Museo has relative strong stroke variations at the joints of its arcs, while Avenir has rather linear strokes.

However, the above-described letter shapes that are most noticeable in the "a", "J" and "k" take some getting used to, or in other words: one has to like them.

On the other hand, the excellent hinting of most Exljbris fonts is uncontested. Both under OS X and Windows 7, 13px is far from being the lower end of the scale thanks to good hinting. This can be clearly seen in the lowercase "e", which has a straight arc in small sizes, while in the larger sizes the arc closely approaches the eye without coming too close.

The x-height is rather high, which is desirable for screen fonts, without being too high and blending in with the uppercase characters as is the case with Vectora, for example. While the italic is probably only a calculated italic, it is

Jos Buivenga, Exljbris 2010, distributed by Exljbris

Rating
(max. ★★★★★)

Hinting:
★★★★★
Glyph shape:
★★★★★
X-height:
★★★★
OS consistency:
★★★★★
Small sizes:
★★★★★
Large sizes:
★★★★★
Tracking:
-

Weights:
100, 300, 500, 700, 900

Styles:
Normal & Italic

Also available at My-Fonts, FontShop and Typekit

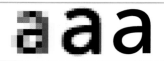

Enlarged depiction of the lowercase "a" of Museo Sans,
based on 8px, 19px and vector (from left to right)

equally well hinted. The same applies to the tracking. It is sufficient and practical, but a little more would not have hurt the application on the Web. Conclusion: Museo is an overall successful font that is well suited for use on the Web.

Museo Sans 100   The five boxing wiza

Museo Sans 100 Italic   Brawny gods just flo

Museo Sans 300   Waltz, bad nymph, f

Museo Sans 300 Italic   Vamp fox held quart:

Museo Sans 500   The five boxing wiza

Museo Sans 500 Italic   Brawny gods just flo

Museo Sans 700   Waltz, bad nymph, f

Museo Sans 700 Italic   Vamp fox held quar

Museo Sans 900   The five boxing wiz

Museo Sans 900 Italic   Brawny gods just fl

Nein, meine Texte les ich nicht, so nicht, stöhnte Oxmox. Er war mit Franklin, Rockwell und dem halbtaxgrauen Panther Weidemann in Memphis (Heartbreak Hotel) zugange. Sie warteten auf die fette Gill, um bei der Bank of Helvetica die Kapitälchen in Kapital umzuwandeln. Oxmox liess nicht locker. Ich fleh euch an, rettet meine Copy, gebt meinem Body nochn Durchschuss! Kein Problem, erbarmte sich Old Face Baskerville, streichelte seinen Hund, zog seine einspaltige Poppl, legte an und traf! (Zeidank nichts Ernstes nurn bisschen Fraktur.) Oxmox: Danke, ist jetzt mit Abstand besser. Derweil jumpte der Fox leise over the Buhl, die sich mal wieder immerdar wie jedes Jahr gesellte. Diesmal war Guaredisch ihr Erwählter, weil seine Laufweite einem vollgetankten Bodoni entsprach und seine ungezügelte Unterlänge ihre Serifen so serafisch streifte, dass sie trotz Techtelmechtelei die magere Futura, jene zuverlässige und gern eingesetzte Langstreckenläuferin, rechtsbündig überholen konnten. Leute, giftelte Tiffany, macht endlich maln Punkt. Und das Komma soll sich gefällixt an die richtige Stelle setzen. Und keine Trennungen. Und nicht zu viele Anschläge heut nacht! Die Goudy war vorbei. Aus

Screenshot (OS X) of a body text as it is depicted on the Web

Open Sans

Nowadays, one comes across Open Sans rather frequently on the Web, as it is one of the most commonly used Google web fonts.

Steve Matteson, 2010, available license-free from Google Fonts

Steve Matteson developed the typeface for Ascender Corp., a Monotype company, which is primarily specialized on fonts for game consoles and whose aim is to "considerably enhance the typographic options for creative professionals." Matteson himself heads the development of the Ascender library.

Open Sans is optimized for use on the Web and ideally suited for this with its open glyphs and neutral shape. According to a statement by Steve Matteson, it is based on Droid Sans, which was developed in 2007 for Android systems. However, Open Sans features wider glyph shapes and italic variations, which benefits the rendering of the font on the Web, as already described above.

Its open counters, which are particularly noticeable in the lowercase "a", "e", "c" and "s", make its rendering on the screen mostly unproblematic. Only the lowercase "g" occasionally causes an increased gray value in individual areas of body copy, which nevertheless hardly affects the harmonious look of the font. Its x-height is only slightly elevated. Its well though-out glyph forms actually do not require a greater height.

The alternative glyphs of the italic styles also ensure good readability even in small sizes. The font features a variety of weights from Light to Extrabold, which ensures great flexibility when used on the Web. In addition, the light, light italic and bold styles of Open Sans are also available in a condensed variation that is excellently suited for use on mobile end devices and similar applications with smaller font rendering. Its condensed variations are primarily distinguished by a very large x-height, ensuring even wider open counters and comfortable readability. In terms of technical implementation, Open Sans is also the flagship of Google. A suitable

Rating
(max. ★★★★★)

Hinting:
★★★★★
Glyph shape:
★★★★★
X-height:
★★★★
OS consistency:
★★★★★
Small sizes:
★★★★★
Large sizes:
★★★★★
Tracking:
★★★★★

Weights:
Light, Regular, Semibold, Bold, Extrabold

Styles:
Normal & Italic

Available from Google Fonts, FontSquirrel and Typekit

Enlarged depiction of the lowercase "a" of Open Sans, based on 8px, 19px and vector (from left to right)

version is provided for each operating system and browser and stored in the cache, substantially decreasing loading times on all pages where the font is also used.

Overall, there is nothing that can be said against Open Sans. It was well though-out and optimized for use on the Web.

Open Sans Light	Open Sans Light AaBbCcDdE(
Open Sans Light Italic	*Open Sans Light Italic AaBbCcD*
Open Sans	Open Sans AaBbCcDdEeFfG{
Open Sans Italic	*Open Sans Italic AaBbCcDdEeI*
Open Sans Semibold	**Open Sans Semibold AaBbC**
Open Sans Semibold Italic	***Open Sans Semibold Italic Aa***
Open Sans Bold	**Open Sans Bold AaBbCcDd**
Open Sans Bold Italic	***Open Sans Bold Italic AaBb(***
Open Sans Extrabold	**Open Sans Extrabold AaB|**
Open Sans Extrabold Italic	***Open Sans Extrabold Italic***

Nein, meine Texte les ich nicht, so nicht, stöhnte Oxmox. Er war mit Franklin, Rockwell und dem halbtaxgrauen Panther Weidemann in Memphis (Heartbreak Hotel) zugange. Sie warteten auf die fette Gill, um bei der Bank of Helvetica die Kapitälchen in Kapital umzuwandeln. Oxmox liess nicht locker. Ich fleh euch an, rettet meine Copy, gebt meinem Body nochn Durchschuss! Kein Problem, erbarmte sich Old Face Baskerville, streichelte seinen Hund, zog seine einspaltige Poppl, legte an und traf! (Zeidank nichts Ernstes nurn bisschen Fraktur.) Oxmox: Danke, ist jetzt mit Abstand besser. Derweil jumpte der Fox leise over the Buhl, die sich mal wieder immerdar wie jedes Jahr gesellte. Diesmal war Guaredisch ihr Erwählter, weil seine Laufweite einem vollgetankten Bodoni entsprach und seine ungezügelte Unterlänge ihre Serifen so serafisch streifte, dass sie trotz Techtelmechtelei die magere Futura, jene zuverlässige und gern eingesetzte Langstreckenläuferin, rechtsbündig überholen konnten. Leute, giftelte Tiffany, macht endlich maln Punkt. Und das Komma soll sich gefällixt an die richtige Stelle setzen. Und keine Trennungen. Und nicht zu viele Anschläge heut nacht! Die Goudy war vorbei. Aus einem üblen Geviert tauchte eine Horde Gemeiner auf, angeführt von einem Versalen. Als sie des Grauwerts anblickig wurden, machten sie auf dem Absatz

Screenshot (OS X) of a body text as it is depicted on the Web

Source Sans Pro

Published by Adobe in 2012, Source Sans Pro is the first open-source typeface that was designed with an eye to its utilization on screen.

It was developed for Adobe by Paul D. Hunt. Source Sans Pro resembles News Gothic and Franklin Gothic by Morris Fuller Benton. During its development, Hunt worked closely with frontend developers who tested the font in their applications. Thanks to the feedback of the immediate users he was able to continuously improve his first versions of the font family.

Upon closer inspection, it quickly becomes apparent that a great amount of attention was paid to the details of the font. The open counters of the basic "a", "c", "e" and "s" resemble those of Open Sans, and are coupled with generous closed counters, which together ensure optimal online readability even in small sizes. Its x-height is only slightly elevated, and it can also benefit from a slight increase of the tracking for copy texts.

Similar to Open Sans, Source Sans Pro features alternative glyphs for italic fonts but does not have a separate condensed font. It also has a well-developed lowercase variation that also includes alternatives such as serif numbers. An extensive language support makes Source Sans Pro also interesting for websites with an international focus, as it contains a set of Vietnamese glyphs and a Latin variation of the Chinese set of glyphs.

Source Sans Pro is available for download from Google Fonts or GitHub in six different weights from ExtraLight to Black each as regular or italic. Anyone who is not interested in self-hosting can receive a CSS link for embedding on websites via Typekit or Google Fonts.

On GitHub one can see that the design and expansion of Source Sans Pro and its glyphs is far from over. Updates and planned extensions are regularly published here.

Paul D. Hunt, 2012, available license-free from Google Fonts or GitHub

Rating
(max. ★★★★★)

Hinting:
★★★★★
Glyph shape:
★★★★★
X-height:
★★★★
OS consistency:
★★★★★
Small sizes:
★★★★★
Large sizes:
★★★★★
Tracking:
★★★★★

Weights:
ExtraLight, Light, Regular, Semibold, Bold, Ultra Bold

Styles:
Normal & Italic

Hosting is also available via Typekit

Enlarged depiction of the lowercase "a" of Source Sans Pro, based on 8px, 19px and vector (from left to right)

For example, recently a mono-spaced version was added along with Greek and Cyrillic sets of glyphs.

Thus, Source Sans Pro is a font that is up to date with the current state of technology and modern demands thanks to constant improvement efforts.

Source Sans Pro ExtraLight	Source Sans Pro ExtraLight /
Source Sans Pro ExtraLight Italic	*Source Sans Pro ExtraLight I*
Source Sans Pro Light	Source Sans Pro Light AaBb
Source Sans Pro Light Italic	*Source Sans Pro Light Italic .*
Source Sans Pro Regular	Source Sans Pro AaBbCcD
Source Sans Pro Regular Italic	*Source Sans Pro Italic AaBl*
Source Sans Pro Semibold	**Source Sans Pro Semibolc**
Source Sans Pro Semibold Italic	***Source Sans Pro Semibold***
Source Sans Pro Bold	**Source Sans Pro Bold Aal**
Source Sans Pro Bold Italic	***Source Sans Pro Bold Ital***
Source Sans Pro Ultra Bold	**Source Sans Pro Ultra B**
Source Sans Pro Ultra Bold Italic	***Source Sans Pro Ultra Bo***

Nein, meine Texte les ich nicht, so nicht, stöhnte Oxmox. Er war mit Franklin, Rockwell und dem halbtaxgrauen Panther Weidemann in Memphis (Heartbreak Hotel) zugange. Sie warteten auf die fette Gill, um bei der Bank of Helvetica die Kapitälchen in Kapital umzuwandeln. Oxmox liess nicht locker. Ich fleh euch an, rettet meine Copy, gebt meinem Body nochn Durchschuss! Kein Problem, erbarmte sich Old Face Baskerville, streichelte seinen Hund, zog seine einspaltige Poppl, legte an und traf! (Zeidank nichts Ernstes nurn bisschen Fraktur.) Oxmox: Danke, ist jetzt mit Abstand besser. Derweil jumpte der Fox leise over the Buhl, die sich mal wieder immerdar wie jedes Jahr gesellte. Diesmal war Guaredisch ihr Erwählter, weil seine Laufweite einem vollgetankten Bodoni entsprach und seine ungezügelte Unterlänge ihre Serifen so serafisch streifte, dass sie trotz Techtelmechtelei die magere Futura, jene zuverlässige und gern eingesetzte Langstreckenläuferin, rechtsbündig überholen konnten. Leute, giftelte Tiffany, macht endlich main Punkt. Und das Komma soll sich gefällixt an die richtige Stelle setzen. Und keine Trennungen. Und nicht zu viele Anschläge heut nacht! Die Goudy war vorbei. Aus einem üblen Geviert

Screenshot (OS X) of a body text as it is depicted on the Web

Ubuntu

Ubuntu is a typeface designed for open and free of charge Linux distribution under the same name by the renowned font studio Dalton Maag.

Dalton Maag became famous for designing the corporate fonts of Vodafone, BMW, Toyota, Sparkasse, and the packaging of McDonald's. Ubuntu was developed for use in the user interface of the operating system as well as in printed documents. In application it appears much larger compared to other web fonts. If we look at the counters of Ubuntu, we can see the reason for this. All glyphs are missing the descenders and ascenders, for example, the ascender of the lowercase "n" (the stem extending upwards from the shoulder). Nevertheless, what does this mean for the x-height?

In most minuscule letters of Ubuntu, the counters have a straight orientation and do not follow a steep arc, as, for example, in Depot and most Antiqua fonts. This way, the bow can be generally designed higher and closed off at the highest (respectively lowest) point of the counter with the brackets almost on the same level. The lowercase "e" for example, barely descends on the bottom towards the baseline, thus ending almost horizontally.

According to Dalton Maag, Ubuntu is based on the humanist shape principle, albeit in a more general way than what we know from textbooks. While the classic, narrow glyphs ("E", "F", "B", "S") are also considerably narrower than wide glyphs such as the "A", they are not even approximately half as wide. Due to the font's humanist style, the designers decided to create true italics instead of resorting to slanted letters. This has considerably improved legibility also in the cursive styles. The counters were opened further, which has an additional positive effect.

As the Ubuntu operating system is used worldwide, it can be noticed that, as opposed to the 750 glyphs that are contained in a standard glyph set, Ubuntu contains approximately 1,200 glyphs. It therefore covers around 200 to 250

Büro Dalton Maag, 2010, available license-free from Ubuntu

Rating
(max. ★★★★★)

Hinting:
★★★★★
Glyph shape:
★★★★★
X-height:
★★★★
OS consistency:
★★★★
Small sizes:
★★★★★
Large sizes:
★★★★★
Tracking:
★★★★

Weights:
Light, Regular, Medium, Bold

Styles:
Normal & Italic

Available on the Ubuntu website or from Google Fonts

Enlarged depiction of the lowercase "a" of Ubuntu, based on 8px, 19px and vector (from left to right)

languages and can be used by around 3 billion people.

In line with the open-source concept of Ubuntu, the complete typeface is available for download on the Ubuntu site as an open-source font free of charge. The font is also available via Google Fonts.

Ubuntu is one of those fonts that have very few disadvantages except for the slightly heavier rendering under OS X. This is fully understandable given the fact that it was developed for its own operating system.

Ubuntu Light	With pangolins dream of qu
Ubuntu Light Italic	*With pangolins dream of qui*
Ubuntu Regular	**With pangolins dream of q**
Ubuntu Regular Italic	*With pangolins dream of qu*
Ubuntu Medium	**With pangolins dream of q**
Ubuntu Medium Italic	*With pangolins dream of q*
Ubuntu Bold	**With pangolins dream of q**
Ubuntu Bold Italic	***With pangolins dream of q***

Nein, meine Texte les ich nicht, so nicht, stöhnte Oxmox. Er war mit Franklin, Rockwell und dem halbtaxgrauen Panther Weidemann in Memphis (Heartbreak Hotel) zugange. Sie warteten auf die fette Gill, um bei der Bank of Helvetica die Kapitälchen in Kapital umzuwandeln. Oxmox liess nicht locker. Ich fleh euch an, rettet meine Copy, gebt meinem Body nochn Durchschuss! Kein Problem, erbarmte sich Old Face Baskerville, streichelte seinen Hund, zog seine einspaltige Poppl, legte an und traf! (Zeidank nichts Ernstes nurn bisschen Fraktur.) Oxmox: Danke, ist jetzt mit Abstand besser. Derweil jumpte der Fox leise over the Buhl, die sich mal wieder immerdar wie jedes Jahr gesellte. Diesmal war Guaredisch ihr Erwählter, weil seine Laufweite einem vollgetankten Bodoni entsprach und seine ungezügelte Unterlänge ihre Serifen so serafisch streifte, dass sie trotz Techtelmechtelei die magere Futura, jene zuverlässige und gern eingesetzte Langstreckenläuferin, rechtsbündig überholen konnten. Leute, giftelte Tiffany, macht endlich maln Punkt. Und das Komma soll sich gefällit an die richtige Stelle setzen. Und keine Trennungen. Und nicht zu viele Anschläge heut nacht! Die Goudy war vorbei. Aus einem üblen Geviert tauchte eine Horde Gemeiner auf, angeführt von einem Versalen. Als sie des Grauwerts anblickig wurden, machten sie auf dem Absatz kehrt

Screenshot (OS X) of a body text as it is depicted on the Web

Embedding of Web Fonts

In print products everything is nice and easy. You simply search for a suitable font and can use it directly. On the Web, an interim step is needed that often intimidates web newcomers.

To be able to use a font, it has to first be embedded on the page. There are two different options for this.

Embedding individual font files
The first option is to download a font and to save it on the server on which the website is located. More precisely, one downloads a web kit of the font that usually contains four fonts. These ensure that the fonts can be displayed by all browsers.

Such a web kit usually contains firstly a True-Type font file TTF (the standard format of font files), secondly an embedded OpenType file (EOT), which is only accessed by the Internet Explorer, and thirdly a Scalable Vector Graphics file (SVG) that is only required for special browsers. The fourth file is the one that is very likely going to replace all the others in the near future, because all the leading font foundries have agree on it and it is supported by all major browsers. This so-called Web Open Font Format is a container format that can contain TrueType, OpenType as well as OpenFont format files.
(for more information see the chapter Font Formats, p. 14)

Some free font providers only allow the fonts to be downloaded in the TrueType or Open-Type format. They must then first be converted to the remaining of the four file formats. This can be done, for example, using the web font generator by FontSquirrel in which the font file is simply uploaded and a ZIP file containing all formats is generated.

However, this is suitable for free fonts only. Even for these, every user should check the license to find out whether the font is licensed for self-hosting, general Internet use or commercial applications. Otherwise it is considered illegal distributions of fonts as they can be downloaded from the server. Newcomers to the Web should better avoid using this method altogether.

Not all font providers support self-hosting, i.e. uploading fonts to the user's own server. However, anyone who has the opportunity should at least thoroughly consider the advantages and disadvantages that are most important for the user and the project.

If one chooses this option and receives the web kit from the font provider it must be downloaded and stored at an appropriate location on the local server. This can simply be a folder called "fonts" or similar. Next the font must be embedded in the CSS with the command @font-face. Each of the web formats must be stated separately for this purpose. It looks like this on the CSS:

```
@font-face {
font-family: ,helvetica';
src:      url(,../ordner-fonts/helvetica-regular.eot') format(,eot'),
          url(,../ordner-fonts/helvetica-regular.woff') format(,woff'),
          url(,../ordner-fonts/helvetica-regular.woff2') format(,woff2'),
          url(,../ordner-fonts/helvetica-regular.ttf') format(,truetype'),
          url(,../ordner-fonts/helvetica-regular.svg#svgHelveticaRegular') format(,svg');
}
```

The character sequence ../ at the beginning of the line serves to move from the folder in which the CSS is located to a parent folder. In this example, the folder and data structure would be as follows:

```
ordner-meine-seite
        ordner-css
                datei-mein-stylesheet.css
        ordner-fonts
                helvetica.eot
                helvetica.woff
                helvetica.woff2
                helvetica.ttf
                helvetica.svg
```

As we are initially in the folder "css-folder" we use the above character sequence ../ to move to the folder "my-page-folder." The folder can be acessed from there and with it the font files contained in it.

The pound key at the end of the SVG denomination in the CSS is needed as the font cannot be identified without it. However, since SVG is only used by old iOS systems, this file is not really required. WOFF2 is also optional, but should be embedded also, if available. WOFF2 will one day be the improved successor format of WOFF and will gradually become more widely distributed. To find out whether a command or a file that one intends to use is supported, we recommend pages such canisuse.com that feature an overview of the applicable technologies on specific devices.

After it has been specified in the code which font styles are being embedded, the font should be given the attributes font-weight and font-style. Font-weight describes the thickness of the stroke of the font. This can be stated as regular, bold, etc., or as a number, e.g. 500. This information is always found on the website of the font provider. Font-style indicates if the font is in italics or normal. One example would therefore be:

```
font-weight: bold
font-style: italic
```

While this information is not necessary in technical terms, it considerably facilitates the handling. If, for example, two fonts of a typeface are embedded later on one of these two settings can be used to change the presentation of the font. Embedding via @font-face has to be repeated this way for every font used on the page. It is therefore not enough to embed a typeface once, instead every font must be individually registered in the code.

Embedding via link

The second option for embedding fonts is possibly the most frequently used –
via a link provided by the font vendor. This link is then embedded either
through an import command on the style sheet or in the <head> section of
the HTML document.

The received link or link kit differs from one provider to the next. At Typekit,
for example, a JavaScript block is provided:

```
<script src="//use.typekit.net/abcdefgh.js"></script>
<script>try{Typekit.load();}catch(e){}</script>
```

At Google Fonts there is a link to a style sheet containing the server locations of the individual files on the Google server. In the HTML file, this would
look as follows:

```
<head>
        <script src="//use.typekit.net/abcdefgh.js">
        </script>
        <script>try{Typekit.load();}catch(e){}</script>
        <link href='http://fonts.googleapis.com/
          css?family=Open+Sans' rel='stylesheet'
          type='text/css'>
</head>
<body>
...
</body>
```

Both ways of embedding have the same effect, the only difference being that the link variation provided by Google can also be registered via a @import in the CSS. It looks as follows in the CSS document:

```
@import url(‚http://fonts.googleapis.com/css?family=Open+Sans');
```

Similar to the self-hosting variation, link or script embedding has some advantages and disadvantages. When purchasing the license of a font for online embedding from a vendor, the font is not really owned, only leased. This leasing is subject to specific conditions such as page views limitation or time-based licenses. If there are problems with the payment or if the subscription expires, the font becomes simply unavailable and is replaced by a system font. *(for more information see the chapter Providers and Licenses, p. 30)*

On the other hand, this type of embedding allows the provider to continuously improve the font. Usually this does not involve changing the look of the font but improving the technology. Google, for example, provides not only five but up to forty font files. These address different operating systems and end devices and ensure that the user's font is updated once a year. The font update saves the font in the web cache of the user's browser, which reduces loading times. For example, Open Sans, which is used on many pages, does not have to be newly loaded every time but remains available until the user deletes the web cache or the license lease expires. It is already loaded when the browser is restarted in the future. This is a great advantage, especially for mobile devices that still have limited data volumes.

The subscription services are particularly interesting for start-ups and small design offices. Many vendors offer low-cost subscriptions that give users a free choice of a vast range of fonts. In most cases, however, the prices for licenses are based on page views per month. *(for more information see the chapter Providers and Licenses, p. 30)*

Self-hosting is particularly interesting for free fonts or the fonts are used on the websites of major companies with large budgets. Most vendors offer companies special offers for using a font without maximum page views and thus hosting it themselves. This often pays off as the font can be used on several pages of the company as well as mobile apps or other end devices. For private persons, this variation offers the advantage that embedding is only required once and the link does not have to be embedded on every page in the <head> section of the HTML. However, users working with a PHP framework such as Symfony, can avoid multiple embedding as in this case it is enough to simply program the page header once and then link it to all other pages.

In general, when it comes to loading times it is always better to centrally define contents at a single location instead of repeating the embedding for every page. Otherwise, when the page is reloaded all external contents, such as fonts, have to be reloaded. This is why this type of embedding is more efficient in terms of loading times. In terms of handling, the main deciding factors are personal pre-ferences and the technical requirements of the project.

Both methods therefore have pros and cons, but their outcome is the same – they provide a font that has been chosen previously to avoid using Arial or Verdana for a website.

Using web fonts in e-mails

To put the plain truth up front: e-mails are the nightmare of all web developers and their technical possibilities are comparable to those of the year 2000. The use of web fonts in e-mails is therefore rather difficult and limited. Most importantly, using web fonts in e-mails is only possible for providers who offer a .css code. This code must be imported and entered prior to entering the actual content.

In addition, for every used font, a <font> tag must be inserted that encloses the respective element. This element can be the cell of a table **<td>**, a headline element **<h1>**, **<h2>**, a paragraph element **<p>**, a text markup **<span>** or a link element **<a>**, etc. It would be used as follows:

```
<style>
        @import url(http://fonts.googleapis.com/css?family=Open+Sans:400);
</style>
```

However, this is only recommended for experienced web developers as the @-import function is not supported by all clients and it can be very difficult to test on which e-mail clients it does not function. This is why the recommendation here unfortunately is to continue using the core fonts that are installed on all devices and apply so-called fallbacks such as serif or sans-serif. The fallbacks make sure that in case a font does not load, another available serif or sans-serif font is used. In an e-mail, this would look as follows:

```
<span style="margin-left:15px; font-size:14px; color:#ffffff; line-height: 1.4;">
        <font face="'Open Sans Condensed'">
                Text in a font of my choosing
        </font>
</span>
```

It can be concluded that in the area of web fonts we are still far from the technological status that we would like to have as users. While there are continuous
new developments, it may take several years until all users have the browsers
and clients that actually support these innovations. In practical application, this
can be seen with Internet Explorer:

```
<span style="font-family:'Open Sans', ,Helvetica Neue', Helvetica, Georgia,
sans-serif;margin-left:15px; font-size:14px; color:#ffffff; line-height: 1.4;">
        Text in a font of my choosing, with a fallback font
</span>
```

The most current and last version of Internet Explorer is IE11 and its successor
Microsoft Edge has already been released. Yet there are large corporations that
still have Internet Explorer 8 (IE8) on all company computers. IE8 was published
in 2008 and neither supports HTML5 nor CSS3.

With e-mail clients this lack of initiative when it comes to updates is even more
prevalent, because, whereas browsers can update automatically or updates
require only a few clicks, e-mail clients must be downloaded and installed and
all e-mail accounts must be registered again. It is well known that this can be
very elaborate and annoying.

We will therefore have to live for quite some time with clients and browsers that
do not support everything that is currently technically possible.

Tools for Web Typography

To successfully apply typography on the Web, it is helpful to be familiar with some tools that are useful for the design and implementation and that make the whole topic more palpable.

Typetester.org

Since 2005, the site www.typetester.org has been one of the best addresses on the Web for creating a preview of web fonts. It allows viewing and comparing various web fonts of different providers directly on the Web. As opposed to many sites of providers, it allows adjustment of the precise settings that determine the final readability of a font.

Often it is only possible to see individual styles of a font in a few lines of random dummy text in black on white. Besides the fact that a dummy text can only be used to judge a font if it is written in the language in which it will be used later, the parameters of a font are our most powerful weapon in web typography. After all, line spacing, word spacing, letter spacing, size, color and other factors can contribute to upgrading an entire website. At typetester.org all these settings can be applied immediately on the page, using fonts by Typekit, Adobe Edge Web Fonts and Google Fonts. If all settings are satisfactory to the designer, the entire set up can be simply exported as a CSS class. At the time of writing of this book, however, the site is undergoing a major makeover as its look and functions are being redesigned.

Currently, the full scope of the page is only available to beta users, but it seems to have some promising new features and some additional new functions plus the old ones.

Most importantly, it is now possible to render fonts in headline size to make clear statements regarding the characteristics of each font when it is used in large sizes.

Typetester has become so firmly embedded in web typography that some of the large font providers already integrate the tool in their websites. For example, Typekit has integrated Typetester in its font selection and the size of fonts can be changed and displayed by a scroll bar, even using a personalized dummy text.

Selection menu of Typetester.org

Whatfont browser plug-in

Web developers (web programmers) are usually quickly able to find out which font with what settings is used on any website. The developer tools of the concerned browser indicate the concerned parameters to the trained eye. For all those that are not experts in HTML and CSS it is more difficult to retrieve this type of information.

For them, and also for developers, the browser plug-in Whatfont is of interest. It can be installed in almost all current browsers via the respective add-on page and summarizes at a single glance the typeface, font style, size, line spacing and provider of the font. After its activation, a simple click on the font in the browser provides the key answers regarding the typography of the concerned page. The plug-in is available free of charge at typerendering.com.

Screenshot Whatfont plug-in in use

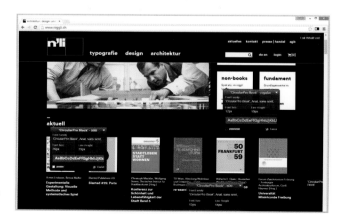

Webfonter.fontshop.com and Typewonder.com

These websites essentially provide the same functions for different providers and differ only in their details. Both simulate the use of a pre-selected web font on an arbitrary or own website. Webfonter is the further development of FontFonter by FontShop and has for many years been the prime example of services of this type. Typewonder accesses Google web fonts and offers similar services as Typetester by Typetester.com. Typewonder also offers the <link> tag at the end, which is required for embedding the font, as well as initialization in CSS as a code snippet.

Webfonter in turn transforms any website into a testing ground for FontShop web fonts. The font of the page can be changed at will and the program even differentiates between headline and body fonts. As opposed to other services, these can be set separately from each other. Unlike other services, the fonts are not listed alphabetically but can be searched in the categories serif, sans serif, slab, script, display and black letter. All this is possible while remaining on the test website.

Webfonter can be used as a bookmark, a plug-in, or a classic web page, and is thus constantly available. Even though the concentration on FontShop fonts seems a bit limited, it includes many classic fonts, which distinguishes Webfonter from the other alternatives.

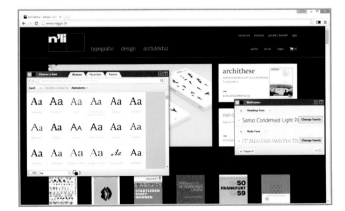

Screenshot with selection windows of Webfonter on the Niggli website

Typerendering.js

In web typography, the transition from web developer to designer is often not clearly demarked. It is therefore very important for both sides to be aware of the tasks of the other side and what possibilities exist. With this JavaScript plug-in it is possible to eliminate the differences created by the various operating systems when rendering the font on the pixel raster. It thus allows introducing rendering commands specifically addressing OS X and Windows on the CSS file created by the plug-in.

This way, a font does not look a few degrees lighter under Windows than it does under OS X.

In short, Typerendering.js is a plug-in that allows the developer to render typography to meet the request of the designer. To achieve this, however, both parties must be aware of the problem and have experience in dealing with it.

Typewolf.com

Compared to the other tools presented here, the site Typewolf.com is more of a resource than a tool but just as useful when it comes to selecting fonts. Similar to many other sites, Typewolf offers an overview of contemporary distinguished website designs and highlights the current state of the art in the area of web design. The main focus is on the typography of the sites. In the overview, the used fonts are already presented together with the name of the site, which is very useful in the design phase in particular. This often reveals fonts that are not included in the favorite fonts category of major providers and typographic trends can already be recognized by recurring font names.

Typecast.com

Many web developers are not very enthusiastic about "what you see is what you get" editors (WYSIWYG editors) such as Dreamweaver or AdobeMuse. One of the main drawbacks of WYSIWYG editors is that they usually generate code that is only machine-readable and not logical to human beings. Similarly, it is very tedious for developers to work only with Photoshop or similar files because this means that during programming they must detect the individual HTML elements (h1, h2, p, etc.) for headlines and paragraphs, without having received logical templates by the designers.

Typecast attempts to bridge this gap precisely and can almost be considered to be the online variation of InDesign. However, as opposed to InDesign and the other WYSIWYG editors, it only offers a preview and not a fully generated website.

An empty platform is available for inserting text that can then be edited in segments or globally. If the text is copied from another website, even HTML elements such as headlines, paragraphs, links, etc. are kept intact. These can then be quickly and easily styled individually. Even though Typecast is operated by Monotype, these elements can utilize the fonts of all the large providers (including Typekit, MyFonts, Fonts.com, Google Fonts, and others).

The completed layout can then be exported as an image file or seen as a link on various browsers and devices. However, the distinguishing feature of Typecast is the fact that it automatically generates a style guide for the page. It displays all used fonts in their respective sizes, colors and individual classes, which is ideally suited for providing web developers with quick access to this data.

If Typecast is used for visualization after the actual layouts have been created in Photoshop or a similar program, then the transfer of the basic elements only takes a few minutes and considerably facilitates the implementation of the page. It also offers designers a good opportunity to clarify the hierarchy within the font on the website. In Photoshop in particular it is often not clear whether a font or a size is used only once or on a regular basis.

In conclusion, it can be said that there are many sites and plug-ins that attempt to support designers and web developers in their work. It is up to everyone individually to decide which ones to use in their personal work flow. To remain up to date, it is important to always keep one's eyes and ears open and to keep up with social networks and news sites about this fascinating topic.

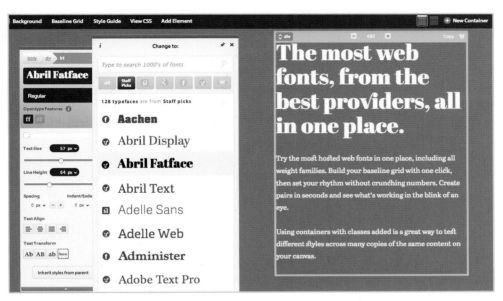

Screenshot Typecast editor

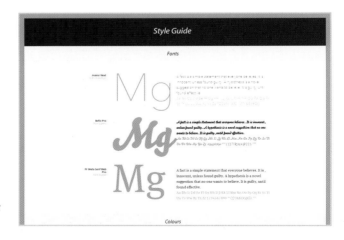

Screenshot Typecast
style guide

Responsive Typography

Print designers are used to the fact that the content they wrap in the layout actually ends up the same way on paper. However, on the Web this is totally different as designing a single layout is only the first step. To ensure that a website looks good on all devices with which users may later on access it, the designer needs to do some preliminary work.

It is important for the designer to recognize the differences among the individual devices and to react accordingly. Design matched to the device of the user is known as Responsive Web Design, or RWD for short. Its aim is to conveniently present the contents on all types of media. For example, mobile websites should not presuppose that the user will be zooming in on the content, but they should also not prevent zooming in. While space may be fully utilized on desktops, it has to be used more efficiently on tablets and laptops.

Therefore, a website should offer at least one size for smartphones, one for tablets, and one for desktop PCs. Intermediate sizes for devices such as laptops and phablets can also be included if desired. Whether these sizes are clearly distinguished from each other and the contents enlarged or reduced in a series of steps, or whether a flexible layout is used that optimally adjusts itself to the available screen, depends on a number of factors:

Behavior of the website of the berlin based agency department one; www.departmentone.com

Factor 1: Time

Three clearly distinguished website sizes are comparatively easy to program. However, they only work if this fact is included in and supported by the layout from the outset. A flexible layout is relatively more elaborate to program and therefore requires more designing effort during the actual programming. Frequently, adjustments need to be made during implementation and carried out spontaneously by the concerned web developer, as often there are no suitable templates to use.

Factor 2: Expertise

For designers the first variation requires more effort as they have to produce at least three different views of every page when handing over their design to the programmers. Programmers on the other hand, can process these layouts one by one and fully focus on the implementation. If the designer does not have much experience in the process, then it becomes clear up ahead that some points need to be improved during programming. Typical examples are the sizes of elements that can be integrated.

For programmers the second variation requires more effort as they often have to work with exceptions and usually have to newly define individual breakpoints, so-called media queries for every sub-page. These provide the browser with the information from which size, alignment, or resolution it should switch to another layout. In this variation, programmers often act as designers as basic elements for the use on mobile devices, such as buttons and navigation elements, often have to be designed from scratch.

Factor 3: Usage

In principle the rule of thumb is that an increasing number of users with different devices and browsers visit the page the longer it is online. As a result, if there is a limited number of firmly defined layout sizes there will be wasted space or too narrow spaces on some devices. However, if the site is intended for a very short period of time, such as the duration of a promotion campaign, the use of limited sizes can save a great amount of time.

It is also important to be aware of the target user group and its behavior. The portfolio of designers, for example, is usually seen by department heads, project managers, or potential customers at their workplace. i.e. their work computers. In this case, special focus should be on the desktop presentation and maybe a differentiation between large and small monitors.

In contrast, the information on a news portal or a marketing campaign is usually read on the go. This is why in these cases the mobile application deserves a bigger focus. In both extreme cases it is important to offer at least a rudimentary view for the other possible devices.

Responsive approach

The term "graceful degradation" has been established to describe the process of responsive adjustment. Its basis is a desktop page that is carefully scaled back to suit mobile devices. This is primarily due to the fact that most commercial websites that are developed in the agency environment are evaluated by decision makers using desktop computers. Unfortunately, this is also often the case when it comes to a website whose target group primarily uses mobile devices. In the agency environment this still is currently the most efficient way.

This approach is countered by the "mobile first" approach, which is also known as "progressive enhancement." The idea behind it is to set up the design as basic as possible and to forego external plug-ins or similar features. These are then added one by one as the bandwidth and resolution increase. While this leads to the best and most efficient results, it requires a great amount of planning as all aims and functions must be clearly defined from the outset. This way, the page does not have to be redesigned during programming to add desktop features.

But now let us turn to our actual topic – typography for various devices. As the examples show, the RWD is based on successful ahead planning. This is because before the typography as such is changed it has to be clear which elements are supposed to change. These include:

Enlarged menu of the desktop view and menu of the smartphone version, www.departmentone.com

Buttons

These should be easy to use even for big fingers without clicking other elements by mistake.

Menus

In addition to the same adjustments as the buttons, it is extremely important that any type of mouseover effect is removed from the navigation.

Headlines

In RWD these can usually be a bit smaller than on the large devices.

Body text

Here the adjustments are not as dramatic as for the other elements, but a well adjusted body text is already half the ticket. To optimally adjust the typography of body texts and headlines, it is expedient to read the line lengths on the two key smartphone sizes of 320px and 360px. While these can be shorter than the standard 50 to 80 characters of print products, they should nevertheless render more than just three words per line.

As smartphones are almost exclusively held in the hand, the distance between the user and the device is usually less than to a computer monitor. This is why the font can be used in a smaller size. It is also worthwhile to switch to a condensed variation so that the reader's flow is not constantly interrupted by line breaks. The further the reader is removed from the device, the larger the font size can be to equalize this. The distance to large devices is usually greater than to compact smartphones. After all, who likes to sit in the front row at the movies?

A renowned web developer conceived an example page a few years ago whose font was based on the distance of the user to the screen as measured by a webcam. However, until this type of automatic recognition is implemented on a large scale, designers and web developers have to make do with estimating the optimal sizes and distances and adjusting the layout accordingly.

The size is determined via resolution, pixels and alignment, whether vertical or horizontal. Each of these must be handled with great care. This is because while smartphones usually respond to a portrait width (vertical mode width) of 320px or 360px, the majority of them have a resolution of 600px and more. This is where the resolution comes to play, which is determined by commands such as:

```
@media all and (min-device-pixel-ratio: 2) and (max-width: 400px)
```

and combined with the width. If we complement this line by the addition:

```
and (orientation: portrait)
```

we prevent a very small device from using this size for a horizontal alignment as well. This information can therefore be combined at will and is essential for finding out where the content is being viewed at the time. However, there are still conformity issues regarding min-device pixel-ratio. It is therefore recommended to use a command that covers all variations that can be interpreted by all browsers.

```
@media all and (-webkit-min-device-pixel-ratio: 2),
        all and (  min--moz-device-pixel-ratio: 2),
        all and (   -o-min-device-pixel-ratio: 2/1),
        all and (     min-device-pixel-ratio: 2)
```

The exact spelling and specifications are best found online. There are many excellent sites that contain all updates and explain everything in a beginner-friendly way.

At the point of publication of this book, www.css-tricks.com is one of the best sites of the sector. For large monitor widths, JavaScript solutions can be used, for example to divide the content into two columns, which is currently not easy to implement with CSS alone.

Another frequently used solution is JavaScript to call a touch event on the page and in this case allocate a class to all <a> elements of a page. This way, links, independent of resolution and size, can be provided with a heavier font that only appears on touch devices to facilitate clicking. The most important thing to observe is that even if the font is rendered smaller or in a condensed style, the tracking remains wider than common for print. As the contrast between bright white pixels and black RGB pixels is greater than what we are familiar with in the print medium, these fonts tend to become blurry in small sizes. In its iOS Human Interface Guidelines, Apple recommends that text should never be smaller than 11 points. It recommends 17 pt as a standard for reading texts.

It is important to test all optimization measures that are recommended for smartphones, phablets, tablets and laptops on as many browsers, operating systems and devices as possible to ensure that all exceptions are covered and all technologies are functioning.

Microtypography on the Web

Of all points in which print and Web differ from each other, the most relevant is the fact that the options for manipulating the appearance of the text are much more limited online than in the print sector.

Yet microtypography in general denotes exactly this – the editing of a composition after the macrotypography, i.e. the choice of font, size, cut, layout and color, has already been completed. This includes, among other measures, the adjustment of distances between letters (tracking and kerning), the use of mark ups for various passages, or the justification of edges by hyphenation.

Hyphenation

In addition to tracking and kerning, hyphenation is one of the most important tools for changing the appearance of the layout of a text. The omission of hyphens or the addition of hyphens at specific points can considerably improve the look of a layout. On the Web, hyphenation is much more difficult to control and less easily available as in print due to the great variety of end devices. This is also the main reason why many typographers still consider web typography to be lacking in quality. On the Web, hyphenations in copy text is subject to many limitations. For headlines

and specific important words a soft hyphen can be inserted with the command **­** but of course this is not practical for every word on every page. While there are generators who will generate hyphens, their use cannot be recommended. For headlines, however, a soft hyphen is one of the most effective weapons for controlling the layout of the text.

For copy text hyphenation is much more problematic. For example, one of the most widely used browsers since its market launch, Google Chrome does not support hyphenation at all. In Mozilla Firefox and Internet Explorer hyphenation is available via the command **hyphens= auto** in combination with the respective prefixes **-ms-**, **-moz-**, and **-webkit-**. However, they do not offer control of this hyphenation, be it by omitting it in some places or by adding new soft hyphens in others. The hyphenation also only works if a language is defined in the HTML document via the language attribute **<html lang="en">**.

```
-webkit-hyphens: auto;
   -moz-hyphens: auto;
    -ms-hyphens: auto;
        hyphens: auto;
```

Letter-spacing and tracking

In CSS there is the attribute letter-spacing with which the general tracking of a font can be changed. While this has been implemented since the first CSS specification and is recognized by all browsers in technical terms, there is a considerable problem in its practical application. This is because not all browsers on all operating systems can process subpixel values such as 0.3px, for example. New Chrome versions and Firefox support subpixel values, but again not on all versions on all systems. This drastically reduces the application options and reliability of this command as any subpixel information is ignored if it is not supported by the browser. This means that 0.7px is not suddenly converted to 1.0px, but instead the default setting remains unchanged. If we want the browser to at least display a rounded value, we can simply define this value twice. First with the rounded number and then with the subpixel value. As a result, the first value is simply overwritten and in all instances where the second value is not recognized the first value is applied. Applying this type of letter spacing to a few select letters is only possible if they are in their own **<span>** tag to tell the CSS precisely to which section this change is supposed to be applied.

Ligatures, kerning and small caps

While it is technically possible to use ligatures, kerning and small caps on the Web, this can only be applied to entire sections without individual exceptions.

Even though the CSS command **font-variant-ligatures:common-ligatures** can be used to directly address the common ligatures such as **ff**, **fi**, **fl**, designers should not rely on them being rendered correctly in all sizes on all browsers. Small caps can also be activated via OpenType functions but are just as unreliable. Still, it is not a bad idea to activate ligatures or small caps in sections of a page where it makes sense, such as headlines in large sizes. In older browsers it is highly likely that such changes will not be displayed but modern browsers benefit from such measures. The same applies to kerning commands, small caps, and alternative characters.

Multiple columns

Even though it is not seen very often, using multiple columns in a web layout is currently possible almost without limitations. However, this is a CSS3 feature and must therefore usually include the browser prefix **-webkit-**, **-moz-**, **-ms-**. It is not available for Internet Explorer 8 and 9 as Microsoft has only been implementing CSS3 features since Internet Explorer 10. With browsers that do not support hyphenation or subpixel information for tracking, the text may appear too dense or too porous. If the columns are set a bit wider, i.e. around 90 characters per line, multiple columns can be used almost problem-free on the Web.

Screenshot test page
JavaScript test

JavaScript manipulation

For microtypography there is a whole range of JavaScript plug-ins that are very easy to install, yet can only affect the layout in a very limited way. Simply stated, there are two types of plug-ins: those that change the font size and those that allow the designer to change the line spacing and tracking of individual letters. The plug-in Flowtype.js is a tool for changing the font size. It adjusts fonts to specific browser or monitor widths. If the designer, for example, defines a minimum size for 600px and less and a maximum size for 1000px and more, the text is adjusted between the two sizes. For example, with the help of **\<br\>** elements for monitors, text can be laid out for 1000px or larger, given that the layout width stays constant from here and only the background width increases. This formatting remains in place down to a size of 600px, with the font only decreasing proportionally while the line length remains constant. However, from 600px, the hyphens must be masked again in the concerned element. This requires slightly more experience in working with HTML.

For the second type of manipulation, kerning.js and lettering.js are the main applied tools. Both allow the styling of individual characters, i.e. providing them with design information on the style sheet (CSS). However, only the locations of the characters can be designed this way and not specific characters in the entire documents (for example, every "a"). This is why these plug-ins are the most interesting to use for headlines. As both plug-ins provide every character with its own **\<span\>** element, it is recommended to use them rather sparingly for overview and compatibility reasons.

For headlines, on the other hand, it is possible to separately design every first, second, third or last word (or other intervals) of all headlines. This way, it is not necessary to provide every headline manually and separately with a span, which makes the plug-in also interesting for working with content management systems. Another advantage is the fact that individual characters can be enlarged, rotated or otherwise manipulated. It should be noted, however, that both plug-ins place spans around all HTML text elements to which they are applied. If, for example, they are used for a headline element, this would also include all spaces and tabs. It is therefore recommended not to include organizing tabs and spaces in the concerned HTML elements when working with these scripts.

In conclusion it can be said that web microtypography is considerably lagging behind web typography in terms of functionality. The tricks stated here at least offer some options for going a little deeper than the standard web typography tools.

Glossary

1: Bit
A bit (short for binary digit) is a measuring unit for digitally stored and transmitted data.

2: CSNet
CSNet (Computer Science Network) was a computer network established in 1981. It was initiated by the National Science Foundation and is considered to be the predecessor of the Internet.

3: Optomechanics
Optomechanics (derived from optics and mechanics) is used for products and processes in which optical and precision mechanics components are used together.

4: Geo-local
Location tracking

5: Hypermedia
Hypermedia is a variation of the term hypertext with an emphasis on the multimedia aspect.

6: Bitstream
Established in 1981, it was the world's first independent digital type foundry. It was acquired by Monotype in 2012 and has been incorporated into the Monotype libraries.

7: FontShop AG
FontShop was established in 1989 by Joan and Erik Spiekermann. It is one of the large manufacturer-independent digital type retailers. Its activities also include the organization of design conferences such as the TYPO Berlin.

8: Linotype
Initially, "Linotype" was the product name of the typesetting machine introduced in 1886. In 1890 the product name "Linotype" was used for the first time as part of the company name. The former Linotype GmbH currently operates under the name "Monotype GmbH" and distributes and licenses digital fonts.

9: Monotype
Monotype GmbH is a company that distributes and licenses digital fonts and develops printer and display drivers for the rendering of digital fonts, especially under commission of well-known manufacturers of operating systems or mobile devices.

10: Berthold AG
The H. Berthold AG company was established in 1858. Initially, the company produced parts for printing presses with movable letters. Subsequently it turned to type and in the 1920s it evolved into the world's largest type foundry. Later H. Berthold AG also manufactured equipment for phototypesetting while the manufacturing of fonts remained a core business of the company. In 1993 the company was dissolved due to excessive financial troubles.

11: Emigre
Emigre Inc. is a US graphic design company and one of the first independent font and software foundries. It was established in 1984 in Berkeley, California, by the designers/typographers Rudy Vander-Lans and Zuzana Licko.

12: Font Bureau
The Font Bureau Inc. is a digital font foundry headquartered in Boston, Massachusetts, USA. The font foundry is one of leading players in the area of font design for magazines and newspaper publishers. Font Bureau was established in1989 by Roger Black, a well-known publication designer, and David Berlow, a renowned font designer.

13: Typekit
Typekit is a service for font embedding on the Web via third-party hosting. It was introduced in 2009 by Small Batch Inc., a company that was established by the inventors of Google Analytics. Typekit has since been purchased by Adobe.

14: Fontdeck
Is a service for font embedding on the Web via third-party hosting. The company was established in 2009 by Jon Tan and Richard Rutter.

15: User Generated Content
Abbreviated as UGC, it is media content that is not generated by the provider of a website, but by its users. The best example of this is Wikipedia.

16: Viewports
Depending on the application, a viewport is the visible section of an image, a video, or the area available for viewing contents.

17: Third-party hosting
Use of the infrastructure of a hosting provider to, for example, embed fonts, which therefore do not have to be installed on the own equipment.

18: HTML5
The fifth version of a hypertext markup language, a computer language for marking up and structuring of texts and other contents of electronic documents, primarily for the World Wide Web.

19: CSS
Cascading Style Sheets is a language for electronic documents. CSS is used to determine the look and formatting of documents written in a markup language. Together with HTML and DOM it is one of the core languages of the World Wide Web.

20: W3C
Short for the World Wide Web Consortium, the main international standards organization for the World Wide Web. The W3C is a membership organization, its founder and director Tim Berners-Lee, is also considered to be the inventor of the World Wide Web. Example of technologies governed by W3C standards include HTML, XHTML, XML, CSS, SVG among others.

21: SVG
Scalable Vector Graphics is the specification recommended by the W3C for the formatting of two-dimensional vector graphics.

22: Unicode
International standard for the encoding of script. It contains a repertoire of every character of the Latin, Arabic, Chinese and any other alphabet as well as special characters such as emoticons, arrows, etc. together with character sequences and numbers.

23: Encoding
Characters are encoded on the Web according to a specific system (e.g. Unicode or ISO-8859-1).

24: IBM
International Business Machines Corporation, established 1924 in the USA, a pioneer of innovations in the technical sector.

25: Netscape
Netscape Navigator was the first widely distributed Internet browser that dominated the Internet in the 1990s.

26: Lesetypografie book
The book "Lesetypografie" (only available in German) is the main work of the renowned book typographers Hans Peter Willberg and Friedrich Forssman. The authors divide texts to which typography is applied into various reading categories and provide precise definitions for the design options of these text types.

27: PHP framework
In the software sector, a framework is a further development of a programming language with additional functions. PHP frameworks such as Symfony or Laravel are specially designed for the use on websites and offer the options of separately embedding files such as headers and footer and inserting translation files for all texts. They also allow the determination of routes on a website at a specific location.

Sources

Images and logos

**Monotype OCR-A
Extended:** Page 7
Source: Specimen of the typeface
OCR-A. The typeface is Monotype
OCR-A Extended 1.80. 01/06/07.
Author: GJo (Wikipedia)

Altair 8800 computer:
Page 7
By Swtpc6800 en:User:Swt-
pc6800 Michael Holley (Transfe-
red from en.wikipedia), [Public
domain], via Wikimedia
Commons

Commodore VIC-20:
Page 8
By Cbmeeks / processed by
Pixel8 (Original uploader was
Cbmeeks at en.wikipedia) [GFDL
(http://www.gnu.org/copyleft/
fdl.html) or CC BY-SA 3.0 (http://
creativecommons.org/licenses/
by-sa/3.0)], via Wikimedia
Commons

**Pixelfont / bitmap font on
an Apple II computer::**
Page 8
By Marcin Wichary (http://www.
flickr.com/photos/
mwichary/2151368358/) [CC BY
2.0 (http://creativecommons.
org/licenses/by/2.0)], via Wikimedia Commons

**The historical logo of the
World Wide Web, created
by Robert Cailliau:** Page 9

By Hell Pé (PNG version); Bibi
Saint-Pol (SVG version)
(Vectorization of Image:WWWlo-
go.png) [Public domain], via
Wikimedia Commons

**Diatype machine of
Berthold AG:** Page 10
By Derivat graph (Own work)
[Public domain], via Wikimedia
Commons

Web 2.0 design: Page 11
von Original by Markus
Angermeier Vectorised and
linked version by Luca Cremonini
[CC BY-SA 2.5 (http://creati-
vecommons.org/licenses/
by-sa/2.5)], via Wikimedia
Commons

**Subpixel rendering
"Sample":** Page 26
Uploaded by Aarchiba,
commonswiki, free source by
public domain

Subpixel rendering "W":
Page 26
By Michael Geary (own work)
[Public domain], via Wikimedia
Commons

**Logo and screenshots
Fonts.com:** Page 31, 33
With the friendly permission of
Vikki Quick, Corporate Communi-
cations Manager, Fonts.com

**Logo and screenshots
MyFonts:** Page 32, 101
With the friendly permission of
Kevin Woodward, Director
E-commerce Development &
Marketing, MyFonts

**Logo und screenshots
Linotype, FontShop:**
Page 34, 35, 102
With the friendly permission of
Ivo Gabrowitsch, Director
Marketing and E-commerce
FontShop and FontFont,
FontFont Library Manager,
Gunnar Malich, LL.M.
Inhouse Legal Counsel,
Monotype

**Logo and screenshots
Adobe Typekit:** Page 36
With the friendly permission of
Nicole Miñoza, Marketing
Manager, Adobe Typekit &
Adobe Type

**Logo and screenshots
FontSquirrel:** Page 38
With the friendly permission of
Joe Manbeck, Customer Support

**Logo and screenshots
Webtype:** Page 39
With the friendly permission of
Paley Dreier, Customer Support

Logo and screenshots Fontstand: Page 43
With the friendly permission of Andrej Krátky, Support, Fontstand

Webtype: Page 50
With the friendly permission of Sam Berlow, General Manager

Agency webpage: Page 61
With the friendly permission of André Lehmann of the agency Achtender

Screenshot Typetester: Page 100
With the friendly permission of Marko Dugonjić, Developer Typetester, Creative and User Experience Director at Creative Nights

Screenshots Typecast: Page 105
With the friendly permission of Paul McKeever, Respective Business Owner Typecast

Enlarged menu of the desktop view and menu of the smartphone version: Page 106, 108
With the friendly permission of www.departmentone.com

Photo of hand with mobile phone: Page 109
Photographer: Jan Vašek
http://jeshoots.com/detail-of-smart-phone/

Screenshots font analysis:
The screenshots of the font analyzes were created with active licenses or trial licenses of the respective providers.

Bembo®
Bembo® is a trademark of The Monotype Corporation registered in the United States Patent and Trademark Office and may be registered in certain jurisdictions.

Gill Sans®
Gill Sans® is a trademark of The Monotype Corporation registered in the United States Patent and Trademark Office and may be registered in certain jurisdictions. - See more at: http://www.monotype.com/de/legal/trademarks?type=G#sthash.bMzhkGMt.dpuf

SkyFonts™
SkyFonts™ is a trademark of Monotype ITC Inc. and may be registered in certain jurisdictions.

Providers + licenses

www.myfonts.com
www.fonts.com
www.linotype.com
www.fontshop.com
www.typekit.com
www.edgewebfonts.adobe.com
www.google.com/fonts
www.fontsquirrel.com
www.webtype.com
www.skyfonts.com
www.fontstand.com

Tools

www. typecast.com
www.typewolf.com
www.chengyinliu.com/whatfont
www.typetester.org
www.typerendering.com
www.simplefocus.com/flowtype
www.kerningjs.com
www.letteringjs.com

408569